BUSINESS ECONOMICS IN A RAPIDLY-CHANGING WORLD

BERNANKE AND GREENSPAN

A DECADE OF SPEECHES FROM JACKSON HOLE, WYOMING

BUSINESS ECONOMICS IN A RAPIDLY-CHANGING WORLD

Additional books in this series can be found on Nova's website under the Series tab.

Additional E-books in this series can be found on Nova's website under the E-book tab.

AMERICA IN THE 21ST CENTURY: POLITICAL AND ECONOMIC ISSUES

Additional books in this series can be found on Nova's website under the Series tab.

Additional E-books in this series can be found on Nova's website under the E-book tab.

BUSINESS ECONOMICS IN A RAPIDLY-CHANGING WORLD

BERNANKE AND GREENSPAN

A DECADE OF SPEECHES FROM JACKSON HOLE, WYOMING

Roy F. Anderson
and
Kenneth Thompson
EDITORS

Nova Science Publishers, Inc.
New York

For permission to use material from this book please contact us:
Telephone 631-231-7269; Fax 631-231-8175
Web Site: http://www.novapublishers.com

Library of Congress Cataloging-in-Publication Data

Bernanke and Greenspan : a decade of speeches from Jackson Hole, Wyoming / editors, Roy F. Anderson and Kenneth Thompson.
p. cm.
Includes index.
ISBN 978-1-62100-912-2 (softcover)
1. Board of Governors of the Federal Reserve System (U.S.) 2. Federal Reserve banks. 3. Monetary policy--United States. 4. United States--Economic policy. I. Bernanke, Ben. II. Greenspan, Alan, 1926- III. Anderson, Roy F. IV. Thompson, Kenneth.
HG2563.B43 2011
332.1'10973--dc23
2011039664

Published by Nova Science Publishers, Inc. † New York

CONTENTS

PREFACE

The Federal Reserve Bank of Kansas City at Jackson Hole, Wyoming, organizes yearly conferences on the long-term economic growth and financial crisis of the United States. This book has compiled a decade of speeches held at these conferences by the chairmans: Bernanke and Greenspan

Chapter 1- Good morning. As always, thanks are due to the Federal Reserve Bank of Kansas City for organizing this conference. This year's topic, long-term economic growth, is indeed pertinent--as has so often been the case at this symposium in past years. In particular, the financial crisis and the subsequent slow recovery have caused some to question whether the United States, notwithstanding its long-term record of vigorous economic growth, might not now be facing a prolonged period of stagnation, regardless of its public policy choices. Might not the very slow pace of economic expansion of the past few years, not only in the United States but also in a number of other advanced economies, morph into something far more long-lasting?

Chapter 2- The annual meeting at Jackson Hole always provides a valuable opportunity to reflect on the economic and financial developments of the preceding year, and recently we have had a great deal on which to reflect. A year ago, in my remarks to this conference, I reviewed the response of the global policy community to the financial crisis.[1] On the whole, when the eruption of the Panic of 2008 threatened the very foundations of the global economy, the world rose to the challenge, with a remarkable degree of international cooperation, despite very difficult conditions and compressed time frames. And when last we gathered here, there were strong indications that the sharp contraction of the global economy of late 2008 and early 2009 had ended. Most economies were growing again, and international trade was once again expanding.

Chapter 3- By the standards of recent decades, the economic environment at the time of this symposium one year ago was quite challenging. A year after the onset of the current crisis in August 2007, financial markets remained stressed, the economy was slowing, and inflation--driven by a global commodity boom--had risen significantly. What we could not fully appreciate when we last gathered here was that the economic and policy environment was about to become vastly more difficult. In the weeks that followed, several systemically critical financial institutions would either fail or come close to failure, activity in some key financial markets would virtually cease, and the global economy would enter a deep recession. My remarks this morning will focus on the extraordinary financial and economic events of the past year, as well as on the policy responses both in the United States and abroad.

Chapter 4- In choosing the topic for this year's symposium--maintaining stability in a changing financial system--the Federal Reserve Bank of Kansas City staff is, once again, right on target. Although we have seen improved functioning in some markets, the financial storm that reached gale force some weeks before our last meeting here in Jackson Hole has not yet subsided, and its effects on the broader economy are becoming apparent in the form of softening economic activity and rising unemployment. Add to this mix a jump in inflation, in part the product of a global commodity boom, and the result has been one of the most challenging economic and policy environments in memory.

Chapter 5- Over the years, Tom Hoenig and his colleagues at the Federal Reserve Bank of Kansas City have done an excellent job of selecting interesting and relevant topics for this annual symposium. I think I can safely say that this year they have outdone themselves. Recently, the subject of housing finance has preoccupied financial-market participants and observers in the United States and around the world. The financial turbulence we have seen had its immediate origins in the problems in the subprime mortgage market, but the effects have been felt in the broader mortgage market and in financial markets more generally, with potential consequences for the performance of the overall economy.

Chapter 6- When geographers study the earth and its features, distance is one of the basic measures they use to describe the patterns they observe. Distance is an elastic concept, however. The physical distance along a great circle from Wausau, Wisconsin to Wuhan, China is fixed at 7,020 miles. But to an economist, the distance from Wausau to Wuhan can also be expressed in other metrics, such as the cost of shipping goods between the two cities, the time it takes for a message to travel those 7,020 miles, and the cost of sending and receiving the message. Economically relevant distances between Wausau and Wuhan may also depend on what trade economists refer to as the "width of the border," which reflects the extra costs of economic exchange imposed by factors such as tariff and nontariff barriers, as well as costs arising from differences in language, culture, legal traditions, and political systems.

Chapter 7- In the spirit of this conference, I asked myself what developments in the past eighteen years--both in the economy and in the economics profession--were most important in changing the way we at the Federal Reserve have approached and implemented monetary policy.

The Federal Reserve System was created in 1913 to counter the recurrent credit stringencies that had so frequently been experienced in earlier decades. As lender of last resort, we had a mandate that, at least viewed from today's perspective, was limited. We did not engage in Systemwide open market operations until the 1920s. And as recently as the 1950s, the framework within which those open market operations were formulated was still being developed. Credit was eased when the economy weakened and tightened when inflation threatened, but largely in an ad hoc manner. As a consequence, the Federal Reserve was perceived by some as often accentuating, rather than damping, cycles in prices and activity. Importantly, however, the surge in prices that followed the removal of wage and price controls after World War II and again after the Korean War kept monetary policymakers wary of the threat of inflation.

Chapter 8- The Federal Reserve will almost surely face as many uncertainties over the next eighteen years as it has over the past eighteen. Technology continues to bring rapid change and, hence, considerable uncertainty, to the global marketplace. Monetary policy, supervision and regulation activities, and payments system operation will need to be calibrated to respond to the influences of that technological change.

Other forces will be at work on the economic environment as well. The inexorable aging of our population will markedly influence the policy milieu in the years ahead. Monetary policy, for example, cannot ignore the potential inflationary pressures inherent in our current fiscal outlook, especially those that could arise in meeting commitments to future retirees. However, I assume that these imbalances will be resolved before stark choices again confront us and that, if they are not, the Fed would resist any temptation to monetize future fiscal deficits. We had too much experience with the dangers of inflation in the 1970s to tolerate going through another bout of dispiriting stagflation. The consequences for both future workers and retirees could be daunting.

Chapter 9- I am pleased to be here this morning to discuss the economic implications of population aging and to provide a general overview of some of the issues that will be covered in much greater detail over the next two days.

The so-called elderly dependency ratio--the ratio of older adults to younger adults--has been rising in the industrialized world for at least 150 years. The pace of increase slowed greatly with the birth of the baby-boom generation after World War II. But elderly dependency will almost certainly rise more rapidly as that generation reaches retirement age.

The changes projected for the United States are not as dramatic as those projected for other areas--particularly Europe and Japan--but they nonetheless present substantial challenges. The growth rate of the working-age population in the United States is anticipated to slow from about 1 percent per year today to about 1/4 percent per year by 2035. At the same time, the percentage of the population that is over 65 is poised to rise markedly--from about 12 percent today to perhaps 20 percent by 2035.

Chapter 10- Uncertainty is not just an important feature of the monetary policy landscape; it is the defining characteristic of that landscape. As a consequence, the conduct of monetary policy in the United States at its core involves crucial elements of risk management, a process that requires an understanding of the many sources of risk and uncertainty that policymakers face and the quantifying of those risks when possible. It also entails devising, in light of those risks, a strategy for policy directed at maximizing the probabilities of achieving over time our goal of price stability and the maximum sustainable economic growth that we associate with it.

Chapter 11- Over the past two decades we have witnessed a remarkable turnaround in the U.S. economy. The aftermath of the Vietnam War and a series of oil shocks had left the United States with high inflation, lackluster productivity growth, and a declining competitive position in international markets.

But rather than accept the role of a once-great, but diminishing economic force, for reasons that will doubtless be debated for years to come, we resurrected the dynamism of previous generations of Americans. A wave of innovation across a broad range of technologies, combined with considerable deregulation and a further lowering of barriers to trade, fostered a pronounced expansion of competition and creative destruction.

In: Bernanke and Greenspan
Editors R. Anderson, et al.
ISBN: 978-1-62100- 912-2

Chapter 1

THE NEAR- AND LONGER-TERM PROSPECTS FOR THE U.S. ECONOMY REMARKS BY BEN S. BERNANKE, CHAIRMAN, BOARD OF GOVERNORS OF THE FEDERAL RESERVE SYSTEM AT THE FEDERAL RESERVE BANK OF KANSAS CITY ECONOMIC SYMPOSIUM JACKSON HOLE, WYOMING

Ben S. Bernanke

Good morning. As always, thanks are due to the Federal Reserve Bank of Kansas City for organizing this conference. This year's topic, long-term economic growth, is indeed pertinent--as has so often been the case at this symposium in past years. In particular, the financial crisis and the subsequent slow recovery have caused some to question whether the United States, notwithstanding its long-term record of vigorous economic growth, might not now be facing a prolonged period of stagnation, regardless of its public policy choices. Might not the very slow pace of economic expansion of the past few years, not only in the United States but also in a number of other advanced economies, morph into something far more long-lasting?

I can certainly appreciate these concerns and am fully aware of the challenges that we face in restoring economic and financial conditions conducive to healthy growth, some of which I will comment on today. With respect to longer-run prospects, however, my own view is more optimistic. As I will discuss, although important problems certainly exist, the growth fundamentals of the United States do not appear to have been permanently altered by the shocks of the past four years. It may take some time, but we can reasonably expect to see a return to growth rates and employment levels consistent with those underlying fundamentals. In the interim, however, the challenges for U.S. economic policymakers are twofold: first, to help our economy further recover from the crisis and the ensuing recession, and second, to do so in a way that will allow the economy to realize its longer-term growth potential. Economic policies should be evaluated in light of both of those objectives.

This morning I will offer some thoughts on why the pace of recovery in the United States has, for the most part, proved disappointing thus far, and I will discuss the Federal Reserve's policy response. I will then turn briefly to the longer-term prospects of our economy and the need for our country's economic policies to be effective from both a shorter-term and longer-term perspective.

Near-Term Prospects for the Economy and Policy

In discussing the prospects for the economy and for policy in the near term, it bears recalling briefly how we got here. The financial crisis that gripped global markets in 2008 and 2009 was more severe than any since the Great Depression. Economic policymakers around the world saw the mounting risks of a global financial meltdown in the fall of 2008 and understood the extraordinarily dire economic consequences that such an event could have. As I have described in previous remarks at this forum, governments and central banks worked forcefully and in close coordination to avert the looming collapse. The actions to stabilize the financial system were accompanied, both in the United States and abroad, by substantial monetary and fiscal stimulus. But notwithstanding these strong and concerted efforts, severe damage to the global economy could not be avoided. The freezing of credit, the sharp drops in asset prices, dysfunction in financial markets, and the resulting blows to confidence sent global production and trade into free fall in late 2008 and early 2009.

We meet here today almost exactly three years since the beginning of the most intense phase of the financial crisis and a bit more than two years since the National Bureau of Economic Research's date for the start of the economic recovery. Where do we stand?

There have been some positive developments over the past few years, particularly when considered in the light of economic prospects as viewed at the depth of the crisis. Overall, the global economy has seen significant growth, led by the emerging-market economies. In the United States, a cyclical recovery, though a modest one by historical standards, is in its ninth quarter. In the financial sphere, the U.S. banking system is generally much healthier now, with banks holding substantially more capital. Credit availability from banks has improved, though it remains tight in categories--such as small business lending--in which the balance sheets of potential borrowers remain impaired. Companies with access to the public bond markets have had no difficulty obtaining credit on favorable terms. Importantly, structural reform is moving forward in the financial sector, with ambitious domestic and international efforts underway to enhance the capital and liquidity of banks, especially the most systemically important banks; to improve risk management and transparency; to strengthen market infrastructure; and to introduce a more systemic, or macroprudential, approach to financial regulation and supervision.

In the broader economy, manufacturing production in the United States has risen nearly 15 percent since its trough, driven substantially by growth in exports. Indeed, the U.S. trade deficit has been notably lower recently than it was before the crisis, reflecting in part the improved competitiveness of U.S. goods and services. Business investment in equipment and software has continued to expand, and productivity gains in some industries have been impressive, though new data have reduced estimates of overall productivity improvement in recent years. Households also have made some progress in repairing their balance sheets--saving more, borrowing less, and reducing their burdens of interest payments and debt. Commodity prices have come off their highs, which will reduce the cost pressures facing businesses and help increase household purchasing power.

Notwithstanding these more positive developments, however, it is clear that the recovery from the crisis has been much less robust than we had hoped. From the latest comprehensive revisions to the national accounts as well as the most recent estimates of growth in the first half of this year, we have learned that the recession was even deeper and the recovery even weaker than we had thought; indeed, aggregate output in the United States still has not returned to the level that it attained before the crisis. Importantly, economic growth has for the most part been at rates insufficient to achieve sustained reductions in unemployment, which has recently been fluctuating a bit above 9 percent. Temporary factors, including the effects of the run-up in commodity prices on consumer and business budgets and the effect of the Japanese disaster on global supply chains and production, were part of the reason for the weak performance of the economy in the first half of 2011; accordingly, growth in the second half looks likely to improve as their influence recedes. However, the incoming data suggest that other, more persistent factors also have been at work.

Why has the recovery from the crisis been so slow and erratic? Historically, recessions have typically sowed the seeds of their own recoveries as reduced spending on investment, housing, and consumer durables generates pent-up demand. As the business cycle bottoms out and confidence returns, this pent-up demand, often augmented by the effects of stimulative monetary and fiscal policies, is met through increased production and hiring. Increased production in turn boosts business revenues and household incomes and provides further impetus to business and household spending. Improving income prospects and balance sheets also make households and businesses more creditworthy, and financial institutions become more willing to lend. Normally, these developments create a virtuous circle of rising incomes and profits, more supportive financial and credit conditions, and lower uncertainty, allowing the process of recovery to develop momentum.

These restorative forces are at work today, and they will continue to promote recovery over time. Unfortunately, the recession, besides being extraordinarily severe as well as global in scope, was also unusual in being associated with both a very deep slump in the housing market and a historic financial crisis. These two features of the downturn, individually and in combination, have acted to slow the natural recovery process.

Notably, the housing sector has been a significant driver of recovery from most recessions in the United States since World War II, but this time--with an overhang of distressed and foreclosed properties, tight credit conditions for builders and potential homebuyers, and ongoing concerns by both potential borrowers and lenders about continued house price declines--the rate of new home construction has remained at less than one-third of its pre-crisis level. The low level of construction has implications not only for builders but for providers of a wide range of goods and services related to housing and homebuilding. Moreover, even as tight credit for some borrowers has been one of the factors restraining housing recovery, the weakness of the housing sector has in turn had adverse effects on financial markets and on the flow of credit. For example, the sharp declines in house prices in some areas have left many homeowners "underwater" on their mortgages, creating financial hardship for households and, through their effects on rates of mortgage delinquency and default, stress for financial institutions as well. Financial pressures on financial institutions and households have contributed, in turn, to greater caution in the extension of credit and to slower growth in consumer spending.

I have already noted the central role of the financial crisis of 2008 and 2009 in sparking the recession. As I also noted, a great deal has been done and is being done to address the causes and effects of the crisis, including a substantial program of financial reform, and conditions in the U.S. banking system and financial markets have improved significantly overall. Nevertheless, financial stress has been and continues to be a significant drag on the recovery, both here and abroad. Bouts of sharp volatility and risk aversion in markets have recently re-emerged in reaction to concerns about both European sovereign debts and developments related to the U.S. fiscal situation, including the recent downgrade of the U.S. long-term credit rating by one of the major rating agencies and the controversy concerning the raising of the U.S. federal debt ceiling. It is difficult to judge by how much these developments have affected economic activity thus far, but there seems little doubt that they have hurt household and business confidence and that they pose ongoing risks to growth. The Federal Reserve continues to monitor developments in financial markets and institutions closely and is in frequent contact with policymakers in Europe and elsewhere.

Monetary policy must be responsive to changes in the economy and, in particular, to the outlook for growth and inflation. As I mentioned earlier, the recent data have indicated that economic growth during the first half of this year was considerably slower than the Federal Open Market Committee had been expecting, and that temporary factors can account for only a portion of the economic weakness that we have observed. Consequently, although we expect a moderate recovery to continue and indeed to strengthen over time, the Committee has marked down its outlook for the likely pace of growth over coming quarters. With commodity prices and other import prices moderating and with longer-term inflation expectations remaining stable, we expect inflation to settle, over coming quarters, at levels at or below the rate of 2 percent, or a bit less, that most Committee participants view as being consistent with our dual mandate.

In light of its current outlook, the Committee recently decided to provide more specific forward guidance about its expectations for the future path of the federal funds rate. In particular, in the statement following our meeting earlier this month, we indicated that economic conditions--including low rates of resource utilization and a subdued outlook for inflation over the medium run--are likely to warrant exceptionally low levels for the federal funds rate at least through mid-2013. That is, in what the Committee judges to be the most likely scenarios for resource utilization and inflation in the medium term, the target for the federal funds rate would be held at its current low levels for at least two more years.

In addition to refining our forward guidance, the Federal Reserve has a range of tools that could be used to provide additional monetary stimulus. We discussed the relative merits and costs of such tools at our August meeting. We will continue to consider those and other pertinent issues, including of course economic and financial developments, at our meeting in September, which has been scheduled for two days (the 20th and the 21st) instead of one to allow a fuller discussion. The Committee will continue to assess the economic outlook in light of incoming information and is prepared to employ its tools as appropriate to promote a stronger economic recovery in a context of price stability.

Economic Policy and Longer-Term Growth in the United States

The financial crisis and its aftermath have posed severe challenges around the globe, particularly in the advanced industrial economies. Thus far I have reviewed some of those challenges, offered some diagnoses for the slow economic recovery in the United States, and briefly discussed the policy response by the Federal Reserve. However, this conference is focused on longer-run economic growth, and appropriately so, given the fundamental importance of long-term growth rates in the determination of living standards. In that spirit, let me turn now to a brief discussion of the longer-run prospects for the U.S. economy and the role of economic policy in shaping those prospects.

Notwithstanding the severe difficulties we currently face, I do not expect the long-run growth potential of the U.S. economy to be materially affected by the crisis and the recession if--and I stress *if*--our country takes the necessary steps to secure that outcome. Over the medium term, housing activity will stabilize and begin to grow again, if for no other reason than that ongoing population growth and household formation will ultimately demand it. Good, proactive housing policies could help speed that process. Financial markets and institutions have already made considerable progress toward normalization, and I anticipate that the financial sector will continue to adapt to ongoing reforms while still performing its vital intermediation functions. Households will continue to strengthen their balance sheets, a process that will be sped up considerably if the recovery accelerates but that will move forward in any case. Businesses will continue to invest in new capital, adopt new technologies, and build on the productivity gains of the past several years. I have confidence that our European colleagues fully appreciate what is at stake in the difficult issues they are now confronting and that, over time, they will take all necessary and appropriate steps to address those issues effectively and comprehensively.

This economic healing will take a while, and there may be setbacks along the way. Moreover, we will need to remain alert to risks to the recovery, including financial risks. However, with one possible exception on which I will elaborate in a moment, the healing process should not leave major scars. Notwithstanding the trauma of the crisis and the recession, the U.S. economy remains the largest in the world, with a highly diverse mix of industries and a degree of international competitiveness that, if anything, has improved in recent years. Our economy retains its traditional advantages of a strong market orientation, a robust entrepreneurial culture, and flexible capital and labor markets. And our country remains a technological leader, with many of the world's leading research universities and the highest spending on research and development of any nation.

Of course, the United States faces many growth challenges. Our population is aging, like those of many other advanced economies, and our society will have to adapt over time to an older workforce. Our K-12 educational system, despite considerable strengths, poorly serves a substantial portion of our population. The costs of health care in the United States are the highest in the world, without fully commensurate results in terms of health outcomes. But all of these long-term issues were well known before the crisis; efforts to address these problems have been ongoing, and these efforts will continue and, I hope, intensify.

The quality of economic policymaking in the United States will heavily influence the nation's longer-term prospects. To allow the economy to grow at its full potential, policymakers must work to promote macroeconomic and financial stability; adopt effective tax, trade, and regulatory policies; foster the development of a skilled workforce; encourage productive investment, both private and public; and provide appropriate support for research and development and for the adoption of new technologies.

The Federal Reserve has a role in promoting the longer-term performance of the economy. Most importantly, monetary policy that ensures that inflation remains low and stable over time contributes to long-run macroeconomic and financial stability. Low and stable inflation improves the functioning of markets, making them more effective at allocating resources; and it allows households and businesses to plan for the future without having to be unduly concerned with unpredictable movements in the general level of prices. The Federal Reserve also fosters macroeconomic and financial stability in its role as a financial regulator, a monitor of overall financial stability, and a liquidity provider of last resort.

Normally, monetary or fiscal policies aimed primarily at promoting a faster pace of economic recovery in the near term would not be expected to significantly affect the longer-term performance of the economy. However, current circumstances may be an exception to that standard view--the exception to which I alluded earlier. Our economy is suffering today from an extraordinarily high level of long-term unemployment, with nearly half of the unemployed having been out of work for more than six months. Under these unusual circumstances, policies that promote a stronger recovery in the near term may serve longer-term objectives as well. In the short term, putting people back to work reduces the hardships inflicted by difficult economic times and helps ensure that our economy is producing at its full potential rather than leaving productive resources fallow. In the longer term, minimizing the duration of unemployment supports a healthy economy by avoiding some of the erosion of skills and loss of attachment to the labor force that is often associated with long-term unemployment.

Notwithstanding this observation, which adds urgency to the need to achieve a cyclical recovery in employment, most of the economic policies that support robust economic growth in the long run are outside the province of the central bank. We have heard a great deal lately about federal fiscal policy in the United States, so I will close with some thoughts on that topic, focusing on the role of fiscal policy in promoting stability and growth.

To achieve economic and financial stability, U.S. fiscal policy must be placed on a sustainable path that ensures that debt relative to national income is at least stable or, preferably, declining over time. As I have emphasized on previous occasions, without significant policy changes, the finances of the federal government will inevitably spiral out of control, risking severe economic and financial damage.[1] The increasing fiscal burden that will be associated with the aging of the population and the ongoing rise in the costs of health care make prompt and decisive action in this area all the more critical.

Although the issue of fiscal sustainability must urgently be addressed, fiscal policymakers should not, as a consequence, disregard the fragility of the current economic recovery. Fortunately, the two goals of achieving fiscal sustainability--which is the result of responsible policies set in place for the longer term--and avoiding the creation of fiscal headwinds for the current recovery are not incompatible. Acting now to put in place a credible plan for reducing future deficits over the longer term, while being attentive to the implications of fiscal choices for the recovery in the near term, can help serve both objectives.

Fiscal policymakers can also promote stronger economic performance through the design of tax policies and spending programs. To the fullest extent possible, our nation's tax and spending policies should increase incentives to work and to save, encourage investments in the skills of our workforce, stimulate private capital formation, promote research and development, and provide necessary public infrastructure. We cannot expect our economy to grow its way out of our fiscal imbalances, but a more productive economy will ease the tradeoffs that we face.

Finally, and perhaps most challenging, the country would be well served by a better process for making fiscal decisions. The negotiations that took place over the summer disrupted financial markets and probably the economy as well, and similar events in the future could, over time, seriously jeopardize the willingness of investors around the world to hold U.S. financial assets or to make direct investments in job-creating U.S. businesses. Although details would have to be negotiated, fiscal policymakers could consider developing a more effective process that sets clear and transparent budget goals, together with budget mechanisms to establish the credibility of those goals. Of course, formal budget goals and mechanisms do not replace the need for fiscal policymakers to make the difficult choices that are needed to put the country's fiscal house in order, which means that public understanding of and support for the goals of fiscal policy are crucial.

Economic policymakers face a range of difficult decisions, relating to both the short-run and long-run challenges we face. I have no doubt, however, that those challenges can be met, and that the fundamental strengths of our economy will ultimately reassert themselves. The Federal Reserve will certainly do all that it can to help restore high rates of growth and employment in a context of price stability.

End Notes

[1] See Ben S. Bernanke (2011), "Fiscal Sustainability," speech delivered at the Annual Conference of the Committee for a Responsible Federal Budget, Washington, June 14, www.federalreserve.gov/newsevents/speech/bernanke20110614a.htm.

In: Bernanke and Greenspan
Editors R. Anderson, et al.
ISBN: 978-1-62100- 912-2

Chapter 2

The Economic Outlook and Monetary Policy Remarks by Ben S. Bernanke, Chairman, Board of Governors of the Federal Reserve System at the Federal Reserve Bank of Kansas City Economic Symposium Jackson Hole, Wyoming

Ben S. Bernanke

The annual meeting at Jackson Hole always provides a valuable opportunity to reflect on the economic and financial developments of the preceding year, and recently we have had a great deal on which to reflect. A year ago, in my remarks to this conference, I reviewed the response of the global policy community to the financial crisis.[1] On the whole, when the eruption of the Panic of 2008 threatened the very foundations of the global economy, the world rose to the challenge, with a remarkable degree of international cooperation, despite very difficult conditions and compressed time frames. And when last we gathered here, there were strong indications that the sharp contraction of the global economy of late 2008 and early 2009 had ended. Most economies were growing again, and international trade was once again expanding.

Notwithstanding some important steps forward, however, as we return once again to Jackson Hole I think we would all agree that, for much of the world, the task of economic recovery and repair remains far from complete. In many countries, including the United States and most other advanced industrial nations, growth during the past year has been too slow and joblessness remains too high. Financial conditions are generally much improved, but bank credit remains tight; moreover, much of the work of implementing financial reform lies ahead of us. Managing fiscal deficits and debt is a daunting challenge for many countries, and imbalances in global trade and current accounts remain a persistent problem.

This list of concerns makes clear that a return to strong and stable economic growth will require appropriate and effective responses from economic policymakers across a wide spectrum, as well as from leaders in the private sector. Central bankers alone cannot solve the world's economic problems. That said, monetary policy continues to play a prominent role in promoting the economic recovery and will be the focus of my remarks today. I will begin with an update on the economic outlook in the United States and then review the measures that the Federal Open Market Committee (FOMC) has taken to support the economic recovery and maintain price stability. I will conclude by discussing and evaluating some policy options that the FOMC has at its disposal, should further action become necessary.

THE ECONOMIC OUTLOOK

As I noted at the outset, when we last gathered here, the deep economic contraction had ended, and we were seeing broad stabilization in global economic activity and the beginnings of a recovery. Concerted government efforts to restore confidence in the financial system, including the aggressive provision of liquidity by central banks, were essential in achieving that outcome. Monetary policies in many countries had been eased aggressively. Fiscal policy--including stimulus packages, expansions of the social safety net, and the countercyclical spending and tax policies known collectively as automatic stabilizers--also helped to arrest the global decline. Once demand began to stabilize, firms gained sufficient confidence to increase production and slow the rapid liquidation of inventories that they had begun during the contraction. Expansionary fiscal policies and a powerful inventory cycle, helped by a recovery in international trade and improved financial conditions, fueled a significant pickup in growth.

At best, though, fiscal impetus and the inventory cycle can drive recovery only temporarily. For a sustained expansion to take hold, growth in private final demand—notably, consumer spending and business fixed investment--must ultimately take the lead. On the whole, in the United States, that critical handoff appears to be under way.

However, although private final demand, output, and employment have indeed been growing for more than a year, the pace of that growth recently appears somewhat less vigorous than we expected. Notably, since stabilizing in mid-2009, real household spending in the United States has grown in the range of 1 to 2 percent at annual rates, a relatively modest pace. Households' caution is understandable. Importantly, the painfully slow recovery in the labor market has restrained growth in labor income, raised uncertainty about job security and prospects, and damped confidence. Also, although consumer credit shows some signs of thawing, responses to our Senior Loan Officer Opinion Survey on Bank Lending Practices suggest that lending standards to households generally remain tight.[2]

The prospects for household spending depend to a significant extent on how the jobs situation evolves. But the pace of spending will also depend on the progress that households make in repairing their financial positions. Among the most notable results to emerge from the recent revision of the U.S. national income data is that, in recent quarters, household saving has been higher than we thought--averaging near 6 percent of disposable income rather than 4 percent, as the earlier data showed.[3] On the one hand, this finding suggests that households, collectively, are even more cautious about the economic outlook and their own prospects than we previously believed. But on the other hand, the upward revision to the saving rate also implies greater progress in the repair of household balance sheets. Stronger balance sheets should in turn allow households to increase their spending more rapidly as credit conditions ease and the overall economy improves.

Household finances and attitudes also bear heavily on the housing market, which has generally remained depressed. In particular, home sales dropped sharply following the recent expiration of the homebuyers' tax credit. Going forward, improved affordability--the result of lower house prices and record-low mortgage rates--should boost the demand for housing. However, the overhang of foreclosed-upon and vacant housing and the difficulties of many households in obtaining mortgage financing are likely to continue to weigh on the pace of residential investment for some time yet.

In the business sector, real investment in equipment and software rose at an annual rate of more than 20 percent over the first half of the year. Some of these gains no doubt reflected spending that had been deferred during the crisis, including investments to replace or update existing equipment. Consequently, investment in equipment and software will almost certainly increase more slowly over the remainder of this year, though it should continue to advance at a solid pace. In contrast, outside of a few areas such as drilling and mining, business investment in structures has continued to contract, although the rate of contraction appears to be slowing.

Although most firms faced problems obtaining credit during the depths of the crisis, over the past year or so a divide has opened between large firms that are able to tap public securities markets and small firms that largely depend on banks. Generally speaking, large firms in good financial condition can obtain credit easily and on favorable terms; moreover, many large firms are holding exceptionally large amounts of cash on their balance sheets. For these firms, willingness to expand--and, in particular, to add permanent employees--depends primarily on expected increases in demand for their products, not on financing costs. Bank-dependent smaller firms, by contrast, have faced significantly greater problems obtaining credit, according to surveys and anecdotes. The Federal Reserve, together with other regulators, has been engaged in significant efforts to improve the credit environment for small businesses. For example, through the provision of specific guidance and extensive examiner training, we are working to help banks strike a good balance between appropriate prudence and reasonable willingness to make loans to creditworthy borrowers. We have also engaged in extensive outreach efforts to banks and small businesses. There is some hopeful news on this front: For the most part, bank lending terms and conditions appear to be stabilizing and are even beginning to ease in some cases, and banks reportedly have become more proactive in seeking out creditworthy borrowers.

Incoming data on the labor market have remained disappointing. Private-sector employment has grown only sluggishly, the small decline in the unemployment rate is attributable more to reduced labor force participation than to job creation, and initial claims for unemployment insurance remain high. Firms are reluctant to add permanent employees, citing slow growth of sales and elevated economic and regulatory uncertainty. In lieu of adding permanent workers, some firms have increased labor input by increasing workweeks, offering full-time work to part-time workers, and making extensive use of temporary workers.

Besides consumption spending and business fixed investment, net exports are a third source of demand for domestic production. The substantial recovery in international trade is a very positive development for the global economy;

for the United States, improving export markets are an important reason that manufacturing has been a leading sector in the recovery. Like others, we were surprised by the sharp deterioration in the U.S. trade balance in the second quarter. However, that deterioration seems to have reflected a number of temporary and special factors. Generally, the arithmetic contribution of net exports to growth in the gross domestic product tends to be much closer to zero, and that is likely to be the case in coming quarters.

Overall, the incoming data suggest that the recovery of output and employment in the United States has slowed in recent months, to a pace somewhat weaker than most FOMC participants projected earlier this year. Much of the unexpected slowing is attributable to the household sector, where consumer spending and the demand for housing have both grown less quickly than was anticipated. Consumer spending may continue to grow relatively slowly in the near term as households focus on repairing their balance sheets. I expect the economy to continue to expand in the second half of this year, albeit at a relatively modest pace.

Despite the weaker data seen recently, the preconditions for a pickup in growth in 2011 appear to remain in place. Monetary policy remains very accommodative, and financial conditions have become more supportive of growth, in part because a concerted effort by policymakers in Europe has reduced fears related to sovereign debts and the banking system there. Banks are improving their balance sheets and appear more willing to lend. Consumers are reducing their debt and building savings, returning household wealth-to-income ratios near to longer-term historical norms. Stronger household finances, rising incomes, and some easing of credit conditions will provide the basis for more-rapid growth in household spending next year.

Businesses' investment in equipment and software should continue to grow at a healthy pace in the coming year, driven by rising demand for products and services, the continuing need to replace or update existing equipment, strong corporate balance sheets, and the low cost of financing, at least for those firms with access to public capital markets. Rising sales and increased business confidence should also lead firms to expand payrolls. However, investment in structures will likely remain weak. On the fiscal front, state and local governments continue to be under pressure; but with tax receipts showing signs of recovery, their spending should decline less rapidly than it has in the past few years. Federal fiscal stimulus seems set to continue to fade but likely not so quickly as to derail growth in coming quarters.

Although output growth should be stronger next year, resource slack and unemployment seem likely to decline only slowly. The prospect of high unemployment for a long period of time remains a central concern of policy. Not only does high unemployment, particularly long-term unemployment, impose heavy costs on the unemployed and their families and on society, but it also poses risks to the sustainability of the recovery itself through its effects on households' incomes and confidence.

Maintaining price stability is also a central concern of policy. Recently, inflation has declined to a level that is slightly below that which FOMC participants view as most conducive to a healthy economy in the long run. With inflation expectations reasonably stable and the economy growing, inflation should remain near current readings for some time before rising slowly toward evels more consistent with the Committee's objectives. At this juncture, the risk of either an undesirable rise in inflation or of significant further disinflation seems low. Of course, the Federal Reserve will monitor price developments closely.

In the remainder of my remarks I will discuss the policies the Federal Reserve is currently using to support economic recovery and price stability. I will also discuss some additional policy options that we could consider, especially if the economic outlook were to deteriorate further.

Federal Reserve Policy

In 2008 and 2009, the Federal Reserve, along with policymakers around the world, took extraordinary actions to arrest the financial crisis and help restore normal functioning in key financial markets, a precondition for economic stabilization. To provide further support for the economic recovery while maintaining price stability, the Fed has also taken extraordinary measures to ease monetary and financial conditions.

Notably, since December 2008, the FOMC has held its target for the federal funds rate in a range of 0 to 25 basis points. Moreover, since March 2009, the Committee has consistently stated its expectation that economic conditions are likely to warrant exceptionally low policy rates for an extended period. Partially in response to FOMC communications, futures markets quotes suggest that investors are not anticipating significant policy tightening by the Federal Reserve for quite some time. Market expectations for continued accommodative policy have in turn helped reduce interest rates on a range of short- and medium-term financial instruments to quite low levels, indeed not far above the zero lower bound on nominal interest rates in many cases.

The FOMC has also acted to improve market functioning and to push longer-term interest rates lower through its large-scale purchases of agency debt, agency mortgage- backed securities (MBS), and longer-term Treasury securities, of which the Federal Reserve currently holds more than $2 trillion. The channels through which the Fed's purchases affect longer-term interest rates and financial conditions more generally have been subject to debate. I see the evidence as most favorable to the view that such purchases work primarily through the so-called portfolio balance channel, which holds that once short-term interest rates have reached zero, the Federal Reserve's purchases of longer-term securities affect financial conditions by changing the quantity and mix of financial assets held by the public. Specifically, the Fed's strategy relies on the presumption that different financial assets are not perfect substitutes in investors' portfolios, so that changes in the net supply of an asset available to investors affect its yield and those of broadly similar assets. Thus, our purchases of Treasury, agency debt, and agency MBS likely both reduced the yields on those securities and also pushed investors into holding other assets with similar characteristics, such as credit risk and duration. For example, some investors who sold MBS to the Fed may have replaced them in their portfolios with longer-term, high-quality corporate bonds, depressing the yields on those assets as well.

The logic of the portfolio balance channel implies that the degree of accommodation delivered by the Federal Reserve's securities purchase program is determined primarily by the quantity and mix of securities the central bank holds or is anticipated to hold at a point in time (the "stock view"), rather than by the current pace of new purchases (the "flow view"). In support of the stock view, the cessation of the Federal Reserve's purchases of agency securities at the end of the first quarter of this year seems to have had only negligible effects on longer-term rates and spreads.

The Federal Reserve did not hold the size of its securities portfolio precisely constant after it ended its agency purchase program earlier this year. Instead, consistent with the Committee's goal of ultimately returning the portfolio to one consisting primarily of Treasury securities, we adopted a policy of re-investing maturing Treasuries in similar securities while allowing agency securities to run off as payments of principal were received. To date, we have realized about $140 billion of repayments of principal on our holdings of agency debt and MBS, most of it prior to the end of the purchase program. Continued repayments at this pace, together with the policy of not re-investing the proceeds, were expected to lead to a slight reduction in policy accommodation over time.

However, more recently, as the pace of economic growth has slowed somewhat, longer-term interest rates have fallen and mortgage refinancing activity has picked up. Increased refinancing has in turn led the Fed's holding of agency MBS to run off more quickly than previously anticipated. Although mortgage prepayment rates are difficult to predict, under the assumption that mortgage rates remain near current levels, we estimated that an additional $400 billion or so of MBS and agency debt currently in the Fed's portfolio could be repaid by the end of 2011.

At their most recent meeting, FOMC participants observed that allowing the Federal Reserve's balance sheet to shrink in this way at a time when the outlook had weakened somewhat was inconsistent with the Committee's intention to provide the monetary accommodation necessary to support the recovery. Moreover, a bad dynamic could come into at play: Any further weakening of the economy that resulted in lower longer-term interest rates and a still-faster pace of mortgage refinancing would likely lead in turn to an even more-rapid runoff of MBS from the Fed's balance sheet. Thus, a weakening of the economy might act indirectly to increase the pace of passive policy tightening--a perverse outcome. In response to these concerns, the FOMC agreed to stabilize the quantity of securities held by the Federal Reserve by re-investing payments of principal on agency securities into longer-term Treasury securities. We decided to reinvest in Treasury securities rather than agency securities because the Federal Reserve already owns a very large share of available agency securities, suggesting that reinvestment in Treasury securities might be more effective in reducing longer-term interest rates and improving financial conditions with less chance of adverse effects on market functioning. Also, as I already noted, reinvestment in Treasury securities is more consistent with the Committee's longer-term objective of a portfolio made up principally of Treasury securities. We do not rule out changing the reinvestment strategy if circumstances warrant, however.

By agreeing to keep constant the size of the Federal Reserve's securities portfolio, the Committee avoided an undesirable passive tightening of policy that might otherwise have occurred. The decision also underscored the Committee's intent to maintain accommodative financial conditions as needed to support the recovery. We will continue to monitor economic developments closely and to evaluate whether additional monetary easing would be beneficial. In particular, the Committee is prepared to provide additional monetary accommodation through unconventional measures if it proves necessary, especially if the outlook were to deteriorate significantly. The issue at this stage is not whether we have the tools to help support economic activity and guard against disinflation. We do. As I will discuss next, the issue is instead whether, at any given juncture, the benefits of each tool, in terms of additional stimulus, outweigh the associated costs or risks of using the tool.

POLICY OPTIONS FOR FURTHER EASING

Notwithstanding the fact that the policy rate is near its zero lower bound, the Federal Reserve retains a number of tools and strategies for providing additional stimulus. I will focus here on three that have been part of recent staff analyses and discussion at FOMC meetings: (1) conducting additional purchases of longer-term securities, (2) modifying the Committee's communication, and (3) reducing the interest paid on excess reserves. I will also comment on a fourth strategy, proposed by several economists--namely, that the FOMC increase its inflation goals.

A first option for providing additional monetary accommodation, if necessary, is to expand the Federal Reserve's holdings of longer-term securities. As I noted earlier, the evidence suggests that the Fed's earlier program of purchases was effective in bringing down term premiums and lowering the costs of borrowing in a number of private credit markets. I regard the program (which was significantly expanded in March 2009) as having made an important contribution to the economic stabilization and recovery that began in the spring of 2009. Likewise, the FOMC's recent decision to stabilize the Federal Reserve's securities holdings should promote financial conditions supportive of recovery.

I believe that additional purchases of longer-term securities, should the FOMC choose to undertake them, would be effective in further easing financial conditions. However, the expected benefits of additional stimulus from further expanding the Fed's balance sheet would have to be weighed against potential risks and costs. One risk of further balance sheet expansion arises from the fact that, lacking much experience with this option, we do not have very precise knowledge of the quantitative effect of changes in our holdings on financial conditions. In particular, the impact of securities purchases may depend to some extent on the state of financial markets and the economy; for example, such purchases seem likely to have their largest effects during periods of economic and financial stress, when markets are less liquid and term premiums are unusually high. The possibility that securities purchases would be most effective at times when they are most needed can be viewed as a positive feature of this tool. However, uncertainty about the quantitative effect of securities purchases increases the difficulty of calibrating and communicating policy responses.

Another concern associated with additional securities purchases is that substantial further expansions of the balance sheet could reduce public confidence in the Fed's ability to execute a smooth exit from its accommodative policies at the appropriate time. Even if unjustified, such a reduction in confidence might lead to an undesired increase in inflation expectations. (Of course, if inflation expectations were too low, or even negative, an increase in inflation expectations could become a benefit.) To mitigate this concern, the Federal Reserve has expended considerable effort in developing a suite of tools to ensure that the exit from highly accommodative policies can be smoothly accomplished when appropriate, and FOMC participants have spoken publicly about these tools on numerous occasions. Indeed, by providing maximum clarity to the public about the methods by which the FOMC will exit its highly accommodative policy stance--and thereby helping to anchor inflation expectations--the Committee increases its own flexibility to use securities purchases to provide additional accommodation, should conditions warrant.

A second policy option for the FOMC would be to ease financial conditions through its communication, for example, by modifying its post-meeting statement. As I noted, the statement currently reflects the FOMC's anticipation that exceptionally low rates will be warranted "for an extended period," contingent on economic conditions. A step the Committee could consider, if conditions called for it, would be to modify the language in the statement to communicate to investors that it anticipates keeping the target for the federal funds rate low for a longer period than is currently priced in markets. Such a change would presumably lower longer-term rates by an amount related to the revision in policy expectations.

Central banks around the world have used a variety of methods to provide future guidance on rates. For example, in April 2009, the Bank of Canada committed to maintain a low policy rate until a specific time, namely, the end of the second quarter of 2010, conditional on the inflation outlook.[4] Although this approach seemed to work well in Canada, committing to keep the policy rate fixed for a specific period carries the risk that market participants may not fully appreciate that any such commitment must ultimately be conditional on how the economy evolves (as the Bank of Canada was careful to state). An alternative communication strategy is for the central bank to explicitly tie its future actions to specific developments in the economy. For example, in March 2001, the Bank of Japan committed to maintaining its policy rate at zero until Japanese consumer prices stabilized or exhibited a year-on-year increase. A potential drawback of using the FOMC's post-meeting statement to influence market expectations is that, at least without a more comprehensive framework in place, it may be difficult to convey the Committee's policy intentions with sufficient precision and conditionality. The Committee will continue to actively review its communication strategy, with the goal of communicating its outlook and policy intentions as clearly as possible.

A third option for further monetary policy easing is to lower the rate of interest that the Fed pays banks on the reserves they hold with the Federal Reserve System. Inside the Fed this rate is known as the IOER rate, the "interest on excess reserves" rate. The IOER rate, currently set at 25 basis points, could be reduced to, say, 10 basis points or even to zero. On the margin, a reduction in the IOER rate would provide banks with an incentive to increase their lending to nonfinancial borrowers or to participants in short-term money markets, reducing short-term interest rates further and possibly leading to some expansion in money and credit aggregates. However, under current circumstances, the effect of reducing the IOER rate on financial conditions in isolation would likely be relatively small. The federal funds rate is currently averaging between 15 and 20 basis points and would almost certainly remain positive after the reduction in the IOER rate. Cutting the IOER rate even to zero would be unlikely therefore to reduce the federal funds rate by more than 10 to 15 basis points. The effect on longer-term rates would probably be even less, although that effect would depend in part on the signal that market participants took from the action about the likely future course of policy. Moreover, such an action could disrupt some key financial markets and institutions. Importantly for the Fed's purposes, a further reduction in very short-term interest rates could lead short-term money markets such as the federal funds market to become much less liquid, as near-zero returns might induce many participants and market-makers to exit. In normal times the Fed relies heavily on a well-functioning federal funds market to implement monetary policy, so we would want to be careful not to do permanent damage to that market.

A rather different type of policy option, which has been proposed by a number of economists, would have the Committee increase its medium-term inflation goals above levels consistent with price stability. I see no support for this option on the FOMC. Conceivably, such a step might make sense in a situation in which a prolonged period of deflation had greatly weakened the confidence of the public in the ability of the central bank to achieve price stability, so that drastic measures were required to shift expectations. Also, in such a situation, higher inflation for a time, by compensating for the prior period of deflation, could help return the price level to what was expected by people who signed long-term contracts, such as debt contracts, before the deflation began.

However, such a strategy is inappropriate for the United States in current circumstances. Inflation expectations appear reasonably well-anchored, and both inflation expectations and actual inflation remain within a range consistent with price stability. In this context, raising the inflation objective would likely entail much greater costs than benefits. Inflation would be higher and probably more volatile under such a policy, undermining confidence and the ability of firms and households to make longer- term plans, while squandering the Fed's hard-won inflation credibility. Inflation expectations would also likely become significantly less stable, and risk premiums in asset markets--including inflation risk premiums--would rise. The combination of increased uncertainty for households and businesses, higher risk premiums in financial markets, and the potential for destabilizing movements in commodity and currency markets would likely overwhelm any benefits arising from this strategy.

Each of the tools that the FOMC has available to provide further policy accommodation--including longer-term securities asset purchases, changes in communication, and reducing the IOER rate--has benefits and drawbacks, which must be appropriately balanced. Under what conditions would the FOMC make further use of these or related policy tools? At this juncture, the Committee has not agreed on specific criteria or triggers for further action, but I can make two general observations.

First, the FOMC will strongly resist deviations from price stability in the downward direction. Falling into deflation is not a significant risk for the United States at this time, but that is true in part because the public understands that the Federal Reserve will be vigilant and proactive in addressing significant further disinflation. It is worthwhile to note that, if deflation risks were to increase, the benefit-cost tradeoffs of some of our policy tools could become significantly more favorable.

Second, regardless of the risks of deflation, the FOMC will do all that it can to ensure continuation of the economic recovery. Consistent with our mandate, the Federal Reserve is committed to promoting growth in employment and reducing resource slack more generally. Because a further significant weakening in the economic outlook would likely be associated with further disinflation, in the current environment there is little or no potential conflict between the goals of supporting growth and employment and of maintaining price stability.

Conclusion

This morning I have reviewed the outlook, the Federal Reserve's response, and its policy options for the future should the recovery falter or inflation decline further.

In sum, the pace of recovery in output and employment has slowed somewhat in recent months, in part because of slower-than-expected growth in consumer spending, as well as continued weakness in residential and nonresidential construction. Despite this recent slowing, however, it is reasonable to expect some pickup in growth in 2011 and in subsequent years. Broad financial conditions, including monetary policy, are supportive of growth, and banks appear to have become somewhat more willing to lend. Importantly, households may have made more progress than we had earlier thought in repairing their balance sheets, allowing them more flexibility to increase their spending as conditions improve. And as the expansion strengthens, firms should become more willing to hire. Inflation should remain subdued for some time, with low risks of either a significant increase or decrease from current levels.

Although what I have just described is, I believe, the most plausible outcome, macroeconomic projections are inherently uncertain, and the economy remains vulnerable to unexpected developments. The Federal Reserve is already supporting the economic recovery by maintaining an extraordinarily accommodative monetary policy, using multiple tools. Should further action prove necessary, policy options are available to provide additional stimulus. Any deployment of these options requires a careful comparison of benefit and cost. However, the Committee will certainly use its tools as needed to maintain price stability--avoiding excessive inflation or further disinflation-- and to promote the continuation of the economic recovery.

As I said at the beginning, we have come a long way, but there is still some way to travel. Together with other economic policymakers and the private sector, the Federal Reserve remains committed to playing its part to help the U.S. economy return to sustained, noninflationary growth.

End Notes

[1] See Ben S. Bernanke (2009), "Reflections on a Year of Crisis," speech delivered at "Financial Stability and Macroeconomic Policy," a symposium sponsored by the Federal Reserve Bank of Kansas City, held in Jackson Hole, Wyo., August 20-22, www.federalreserve.gov/newsevents/speech/bernanke20090821a.htm.

[2] The most recent survey is available on the Board's website at www.federalreserve.gov/boarddocs/SnLoanSurvey.

[3] Data are from the national and income product accounts produced by the Bureau of Economic Analysis, U.S. Department of Commerce.

[4] In April 2010, the Bank of Canada removed the conditional commitment from its statement, and in June 2010, the Bank raised its policy rate and announced a return to its normal operating framework for the overnight rate.

In: Bernanke and Greenspan
Editors R. Anderson, et al.
ISBN: 978-1-62100- 912-2

Chapter 3

AT THE FEDERAL RESERVE BANK OF KANSAS CITY'S ANNUAL ECONOMIC SYMPOSIUM, JACKSON HOLE, WYOMING AUGUST 21, 2009

Ben S. Bernanke

REFLECTIONS ON A YEAR OF CRISIS

By the standards of recent decades, the economic environment at the time of this symposium one year ago was quite challenging. A year after the onset of the current crisis in August 2007, financial markets remained stressed, the economy was slowing, and inflation--driven by a global commodity boom--had risen significantly. What we could not fully appreciate when we last gathered here was that the economic and policy environment was about to become vastly more difficult. In the weeks that followed, several systemically critical financial institutions would either fail or come close to failure, activity in some key financial markets would virtually cease, and the global economy would enter a deep recession. My remarks this morning will focus on the extraordinary financial and economic events of the past year, as well as on the policy responses both in the United States and abroad.

One very clear lesson of the past year--no surprise, of course, to any student of economic history, but worth noting nonetheless--is that a full-blown financial crisis can exact an enormous toll in both human and economic terms.

A second lesson--once again, familiar to economic historians--is that financial disruptions do not respect borders. The crisis has been global, with no major country having been immune.

History is full of examples in which the policy responses to financial crises have been slow and inadequate, often resulting ultimately in greater economic damage and increased fiscal costs. In this episode, by contrast, policymakers in the United States and around the globe responded with speed and force to arrest a rapidly deteriorating and dangerous situation. Looking forward, we must urgently address structural weaknesses in the financial system, in particular in the regulatory framework, to ensure that the enormous costs of the past two years will not be borne again.

September-October 2008: The Crisis Intensifies

When we met last year, financial markets and the economy were continuing to suffer the effects of the ongoing crisis. We know now that the National Bureau of Economic Research has determined December 2007 as the beginning of the recession. The U.S. unemployment rate had risen to 5-3/4 percent by July, about 1 percentage point above its level at the beginning of the crisis, and household spending was weakening. Ongoing declines in residential construction and house prices and rising mortgage defaults and foreclosures continued to weigh on the U.S. economy, and forecasts of prospective credit losses at financial institutions both here and abroad continued to increase. Indeed, one of the nation's largest thrift institutions, IndyMac, had recently collapsed under the weight of distressed mortgages, and investors continued to harbor doubts about the condition of the government-sponsored enterprises (GSEs) Fannie Mae and Freddie Mac, despite the approval by the Congress of open-ended support for the two firms.

Notwithstanding these significant concerns, however, there was little to suggest that market participants saw the financial situation as about to take a sharp turn for the worse. For example, although indicators of default risk such as interest rate spreads and quotes on credit default swaps remained well above historical norms, most such measures had declined from earlier peaks, in some cases by substantial amounts. And in early September, when the target for the federal funds rate was 2 percent, investors appeared to see little chance that the federal funds rate would be below 1-3/4 percent six months later. That is, as of this time last year, market participants evidently believed it improbable that significant additional monetary policy stimulus would be needed in the United States.

Nevertheless, shortly after our last convocation, the financial crisis intensified dramatically. Despite the steps that had been taken to support Fannie Mae and Freddie Mac, their condition continued to worsen. In early September, the companies' regulator placed both into conservatorship, and the Treasury used its recently enacted authority to provide the firms with massive financial support.

Shortly thereafter, several additional large U.S. financial firms also came under heavy pressure from creditors, counterparties, and customers. The Federal Reserve has consistently maintained the view that the disorderly failure of one or more systemically important institutions in the context of a broader financial crisis could have extremely adverse consequences for both the financial system and the economy. We have therefore spared no effort, within our legal authorities and in appropriate cooperation with other agencies, to avert such a failure. The case of the investment bank Lehman Brothers proved exceptionally difficult, however. Concerted government attempts to find a buyer for the company or to develop an industry solution proved unavailing, and the company's available collateral fell well short of the amount needed to secure a Federal Reserve loan of sufficient size to meet its funding needs. As the Federal Reserve cannot make an unsecured loan, and as the government as a whole lacked appropriate resolution authority or the ability to inject capital, the firm's failure was, unfortunately, unavoidable. The Federal Reserve and the Treasury were compelled to focus instead on mitigating the fallout from the failure, for example, by taking measures to stabilize the triparty repurchase (repo) market.

In contrast, in the case of the insurance company American International Group (AIG), the Federal Reserve judged that the company's financial and business assets were adequate to secure an $85 billion line of credit, enough to avert its imminent failure. Because AIG was counterparty to many of the world's largest financial firms, a significant borrower in the commercial paper market and other public debt markets, and a provider of insurance products to tens of millions of customers, its abrupt collapse likely would have intensified the crisis substantially further, at a time when the U.S. authorities had not yet obtained the necessary fiscal resources to deal with a massive systemic event.

The failure of Lehman Brothers and the near-failure of AIG were dramatic but hardly isolated events. Many prominent firms struggled to survive as confidence plummeted. The investment bank Merrill Lynch, under pressure in the wake of Lehman's failure, agreed to be acquired by Bank of America; the major thrift institution Washington Mutual was resolved by the Federal Deposit Insurance Corporation (FDIC) in an assisted transaction; and the large commercial bank Wachovia, after experiencing severe liquidity outflows, agreed to be sold. The two largest remaining free-standing investment banks, Morgan Stanley and Goldman Sachs, were stabilized when the Federal Reserve approved, on an emergency basis, their applications to become bank holding companies.

Nor were the extraordinary pressures on financial firms during September and early October confined to the United States: For example, on September 18, the U.K. mortgage lender HBOS, with assets of more than $1 trillion, was forced to merge with Lloyds TSB. On September 29, the governments of Belgium, Luxembourg, and the Netherlands effectively nationalized Fortis, a banking and insurance firm that had assets of around $1 trillion. The same day, German authorities provided assistance to Hypo Real Estate, a large commercial real estate lender, and the British government nationalized another mortgage lender, Bradford and Bingley. On the next day, September 30, the governments of Belgium, France, and Luxembourg injected capital into Dexia, a bank with assets of more than $700 billion, and the Irish government guaranteed the deposits and most other liabilities of six large Irish financial institutions. Soon thereafter, the Icelandic government, lacking the resources to rescue the three largest banks in that country, put them into receivership and requested assistance from the International Monetary Fund (IMF) and from other Nordic governments. In mid-October, the Swiss authorities announced a rescue package for UBS, one of the world's largest banks, that consisted of a capital injection and a purchase of assets.[1] The growing pressures were not limited to banks with significant exposure to U.S. or U.K real estate or to securitized assets. For example, unsubstantiated rumors circulated in late September that some large Swedish banks were having trouble rolling over wholesale deposits, and on October 13 the Swedish government announced measures to guarantee bank debt and to inject capital into banks.[2]

The rapidly worsening crisis soon spread beyond financial institutions into the money and capital markets more generally. As a result of losses on Lehman's commercial paper, a prominent money market mutual fund announced on September 16 that it had "broken the buck"--that is, its net asset value had fallen below $1 per share. Over the subsequent several weeks, investors withdrew more than $400 billion from so-called prime money funds.[3] Conditions in short-term funding markets, including the interbank market and the commercial paper market, deteriorated sharply. Equity prices fell precipitously, and credit risk spreads jumped. The crisis also began to affect countries that had thus far escaped its worst effects. Notably, financial markets in emerging market economies were whipsawed as a flight from risk led capital inflows to those countries to swing abruptly to outflows.

The Policy Response

Authorities in the United States and around the globe moved quickly to respond to this new phase of the crisis, although the details differed according to the character of financial systems. The financial system of the United States gives a much greater role to financial markets and to nonbank financial institutions than is the case in most other nations, which rely primarily on banks.[4] Thus, in the United States, a wider variety of policy measures was needed than in some other nations.

In the United States, the Federal Reserve established new liquidity facilities with the goal of restoring basic functioning in various critical markets. Notably, on September 19, the Fed announced the creation of a facility aimed at stabilizing money market mutual funds, and the Treasury unveiled a temporary insurance program for those funds. On October 7, the Fed announced the creation of a backstop commercial paper facility, which stood ready to lend against highly rated commercial paper for a term of three months.[5] Together, these steps helped stem the massive outflows from the money market mutual funds and stabilize the commercial paper market.

During this period, foreign commercial banks were a source of heavy demand for U.S. dollar funding, thereby putting additional strain on global bank funding markets, including U.S. markets, and further squeezing credit availability in the United States. To address this problem, the Federal Reserve expanded the temporary swap lines that had been established earlier with the European Central Bank (ECB) and the Swiss National Bank, and established new temporary swap lines with seven other central banks in September and five more in late October, including four in emerging market economies.[6] In further coordinated action, on October 8, the Federal Reserve and five other major central banks simultaneously cut their policy rates by 50 basis points.

The failure of Lehman Brothers demonstrated that liquidity provision by the Federal Reserve would not be sufficient to stop the crisis; substantial fiscal resources were necessary. On October 3, on the recommendation of the Administration and with the strong support of the Federal Reserve, the Congress approved the creation of the Troubled Asset Relief Program, or

TARP, with a maximum authorization of $700 billion to support the stabilization of the U.S. financial system.

Markets remained highly volatile and pressure on financial institutions intense through the first weeks of October. On October 10, in what would prove to be a watershed in the global policy response, the Group of Seven (G-7) finance ministers and central bank governors, meeting in Washington, committed in a joint statement to work together to stabilize the global financial system. In particular, they agreed to prevent the failure of systemically important financial institutions; to ensure that financial institutions had adequate access to funding and capital, including public capital if necessary; and to put in place deposit insurance and other guarantees to restore the confidence of depositors.[7] In the following days, many countries around the world announced comprehensive rescue plans for their banking systems that built on the G-7 principles. To stabilize funding, during October more than 20 countries expanded their deposit insurance programs, and many also guaranteed nondeposit liabilities of banks. In addition, amid mounting concerns about the solvency of the global banking system, by the end of October more than a dozen countries had announced plans to inject public capital into banks, and several announced plans to purchase or guarantee bank assets. The comprehensive U.S. response, announced on October 14, included capital injections into both large and small banks by the Treasury; a program which allowed banks and bank holding companies, for a fee, to issue FDIC-guaranteed senior debt; the extension of deposit insurance to all noninterest-bearing transactions deposits, of any size; and the Federal Reserve's continued commitment to provide liquidity as necessary to stabilize key financial institutions and markets.[8]

This strong and unprecedented international policy response proved broadly effective. Critically, it averted the imminent collapse of the global financial system, an outcome that seemed all too possible to the finance ministers and central bankers that gathered in Washington on October 10. However, although the intensity of the crisis moderated and the risk of systemic collapse declined in the wake of the policy response, financial conditions remained highly stressed. For example, although short-term funding spreads in global markets began to turn down in October, they remained elevated into this year. And, although generalized pressures on financial institutions subsided somewhat, government actions to prevent the disorderly failures of individual, systemically significant institutions continued to be necessary. In the United States, support packages were announced for Citigroup in November and Bank of America in January. Broadly similar into illiquid markets. These forced sales drive down asset prices, increase volatility, and weaken the financial positions of all holders of similar assets, which in turn increases the risks borne by repo lenders and thus the haircuts they demand.[16] This unstable dynamic was apparent around the time of the near-failure of Bear Stearns in March 2008, and haircuts rose particularly sharply during the worsening of the crisis in mid-September.[17] As we saw last fall, when a vicious funding spiral of this sort is at work, falling asset prices and the collapse of lender confidence may create financial contagion, even between firms without significant counterparty relationships. In such an environment, the line between insolvency and illiquidity may be quite blurry.

Panic-like phenomena occurred in other contexts as well. Structured investment vehicles and other asset-backed programs that relied heavily on the commercial paper market began to have difficulty rolling over their short-term funding very early in the crisis, forcing them to look to bank sponsors for liquidity or to sell assets.[18] Following the Lehman collapse, panic gripped the money market mutual funds and the commercial paper market, as I have discussed. More generally, during the crisis runs of uninsured creditors have created severe funding problems for a number of financial firms. In some cases, runs by creditors were augmented by other types of "runs"--for example, by prime brokerage customers of investment banks concerned about the funds they held in margin accounts. Overall, the role played by panic helps to explain the remarkably sharp and sudden intensification of the financial crisis last fall, its rapid global spread, and the fact that the abrupt deterioration in financial conditions was largely unforecasted by standard market indicators.

The view that the financial crisis had elements of a classic panic, particularly during its most intense phases, has helped to motivate a number of the Federal Reserve's policy actions.[19] Bagehot instructed central banks--the only institutions that have the power to increase the aggregate liquidity in the system--to respond to panics by lending freely against sound collateral.[20] Following that advice, from the beginning of the crisis the Fed (like other central banks) has provided large amounts of short-term liquidity to financial institutions. As I have discussed, it also provided backstop liquidity support for money market mutual funds and the commercial paper market and added significant liquidity to the system through purchases of longer-term securities. To be sure, the provision of liquidity alone can by no means solve the problems of credit risk and credit losses; but it can reduce liquidity premiums, help restore the confidence of investors, and thus promote stability. It is noteworthy that the use of Fed liquidity facilities has declined sharply since

support packages were also announced for some large European institutions, including firms in the United Kingdom and the Netherlands.[9]

Although concerted policy actions avoided much worse outcomes, the financial shocks of September and October nevertheless severely damaged the global economy--starkly illustrating the potential effects of financial stress on real economic activity. In the fourth quarter of 2008 and the first quarter of this year, global economic activity recorded its weakest performance in decades. In the United States, real GDP plummeted at nearly a 6 percent average annual pace over those two quarters--an even sharper decline than had occurred in the 1981-82 recession. Economic activity contracted even more precipitously in many foreign economies, with real GDP dropping at double-digit annual rates in some cases. The crisis affected economic activity not only by pushing down asset prices and tightening credit conditions, but also by shattering household and business confidence around the world.

In response to these developments, the Federal Reserve expended the remaining ammunition in the traditional arsenal of monetary policy, bringing the federal funds rate down, in steps, to a target range of 0 to 25 basis points by mid-December of last year. It also took several measures to further supplement its traditional arsenal. In particular, on November 25, the Fed announced that it would purchase up to $100 billion of debt issued by the housing-related GSEs and up to $500 billion of agency-guaranteed mortgage-backed securities, programs that were expanded substantially and augmented by a program of purchases of Treasury securities in March.[10] The goal of these purchases was to provide additional support to private credit markets, particularly the mortgage market. Also on November 25, the Fed announced the creation of the Term Asset-Backed Securities Loan Facility (TALF). This facility aims to improve the availability and affordability of credit for households and small businesses and to help facilitate the financing and refinancing of commercial real estate properties. The TALF has shown early success in reducing risk spreads and stimulating new securitization activity for assets included in the program.

Foreign central banks also cut policy rates to very low levels and implemented unconventional monetary measures. For example, the Bank of Japan began purchasing commercial paper in December and corporate bonds in January. In March, the Bank of England announced that it would purchase government securities, commercial paper, and corporate bonds, and the Swiss National Bank announced that it would purchase corporate bonds and foreign currency. For its part, the ECB injected more than €400 billion of one-year funds in a single auction in late June. In July, the ECB began purchasing covered bonds, which are bonds that are issued by financial institutions and guaranteed by specific asset pools. Actions by central banks augmented large fiscal stimulus packages in the United States, China, and a number of other countries.

On February 10, Treasury Secretary Geithner and the heads of the federal banking agencies unveiled the outlines of a new strategy for ensuring that banking institutions could continue to provide credit to households and businesses during the financial crisis. A central component of that strategy was the exercise that came to be known as the bank stress test.[11] Under this initiative, the banking regulatory agencies undertook a forward-looking, simultaneous evaluation of the capital positions of 19 of the largest bank holding companies in the United States, with the Treasury committing to provide public capital as needed. The goal of this supervisory assessment was to ensure that the equity capital held by these firms was sufficient--in both quantity and quality--to allow those institutions to withstand a worse-than-expected macroeconomic environment over the subsequent two years and yet remain healthy and capable of lending to creditworthy borrowers. This exercise, unprecedented in scale and scope, was led by the Federal Reserve in cooperation with the Office of the Comptroller of the Currency and the FDIC. Importantly, the agencies' report made public considerable information on the projected losses and revenues of the 19 firms, allowing private analysts to judge for themselves the credibility of the exercise. Financial market participants responded favorably to the announcement of the results, and many of the tested banks were subsequently able to tap public capital markets.

Overall, the policy actions implemented in recent months have helped stabilize a number of key financial markets, both in the United States and abroad. Short-term funding markets are functioning more normally, corporate bond issuance has been strong, and activity in some previously moribund securitization markets has picked up. Stock prices have partially recovered, and U.S. mortgage rates have declined markedly since last fall. Critically, fears of financial collapse have receded substantially. After contracting sharply over the past year, economic activity appears to be leveling out, both in the United States and abroad, and the prospects for a return to growth in the near term appear good. Notwithstanding this noteworthy progress, critical challenges remain: Strains persist in many financial markets across the globe, financial institutions face significant additional losses, and many businesses and households continue to experience considerable difficulty gaining access to credit. Because of these and other factors, the economic recovery is likely to

be relatively slow at first, with unemployment declining only gradually from high levels.

Interpreting the Crisis: Elements of a Classic Panic

How should we interpret the extraordinary events of the past year, particularly the sharp intensification of the financial crisis in September and October? Certainly, fundamentals played a critical role in triggering those events. As I noted earlier, the economy was already in recession, and it had weakened further over the summer. The continuing dramatic decline in house prices and rising rates of foreclosure raised serious concerns about the values of mortgage-related assets, and thus about large potential losses at financial institutions. More broadly, investors remained distrustful of virtually all forms of private credit, especially structured credit products and other complex or opaque instruments.

At the same time, however, the events of September and October als exhibited some features of a classic panic, of the type described by Bageh and many others.[12] A panic is a generalized run by providers of short-ter funding to a set of financial institutions, possibly resulting in the failure of c or more of those institutions. The historically most familiar type of pa which involves runs on banks by retail depositors, has been made larg obsolete by deposit insurance or guarantees and the associated governn supervision of banks.[13] But a panic is possible in any situation in w longer-term, illiquid assets are financed by short-term, liquid liabilities, a which suppliers of short-term funding either lose confidence in the borr or become worried that other short-term lenders may lose confidenc Although, in a certain sense, a panic may be collectively irrational, it m entirely rational at the individual level, as each market participant has a incentive to be among the first to the exit.

Panics arose in multiple contexts last year. For example, many fi institutions, notably including the independent investment banks, fin portion of their assets through short-term repo agreements. In repo agre the asset being financed serves as collateral for the loan, and the m amount of the loan is the current assessed value of the collateral less In a crisis, haircuts typically rise as short-term lenders attempt t themselves from possible declines in asset prices. But this individuall behavior can set off a run-like dynamic: As high haircuts make portfolios more difficult, some borrowers may have no option but to

the beginning of the year--a clear market signal that liquidity pressures are easing and market conditions are normalizing.

What does this perspective on the crisis imply for future policies and regulatory reforms? We have seen during the past two years that the complex interrelationships among credit, market, and funding risks of key players in financial markets can have far-reaching implications, particularly during a general crisis of confidence. In particular, the experience has underscored that liquidity risk management is as essential as capital adequacy and credit and market risk management, particularly during times of intense financial stress. Both the Basel Committee on Banking Supervision and the U.S. bank regulatory agencies have recently issued guidelines for strengthening liquidity risk management at financial institutions. Among other objectives, liquidity guidelines must take into account the risks that inadequate liquidity planning by major financial firms pose for the broader financial system, and they must ensure that these firms do not become excessively reliant on liquidity support from the central bank.

But liquidity risk management at the level of the firm, no matter how carefully done, can never fully protect against systemic events. In a sufficiently severe panic, funding problems will almost certainly arise and are likely to spread in unexpected ways. Only central banks are well positioned to offset the ensuing sharp decline in liquidity and credit provision by the private sector. They must be prepared to do so.

The role of liquidity in systemic events provides yet another reason why, in the future, a more systemwide or macroprudential approach to regulation is needed.[21] The hallmark of a macroprudential approach is its emphasis on the interdependencies among firms and markets that have the potential to undermine the stability of the financial system, including the linkages that arise through short-term funding markets and other counterparty relationships, such as over-the-counter derivatives contracts. A comprehensive regulatory approach must examine those interdependencies as well as the financial conditions of individual firms in isolation.

CONCLUSION

Since we last met here, the world has been through the most severe financial crisis since the Great Depression. The crisis in turn sparked a deep global recession, from which we are only now beginning to emerge.

As severe as the economic impact has been, however, the outcome could have been decidedly worse. Unlike in the 1930s, when policy was largely passive and political divisions made international economic and financial cooperation difficult, during the past year monetary, fiscal, and financial policies around the world have been aggressive and complementary. Without these speedy and forceful actions, last October's panic would likely have continued to intensify, more major financial firms would have failed, and the entire global financial system would have been at serious risk. We cannot know for sure what the economic effects of these events would have been, but what we know about the effects of financial crises suggests that the resulting global downturn could have been extraordinarily deep and protracted.

Although we have avoided the worst, difficult challenges still lie ahead. We must work together to build on the gains already made to secure a sustained economic recovery, as well as to build a new financial regulatory framework that will reflect the lessons of this crisis and prevent a recurrence of the events of the past two years. I hope and expect that, when we meet here a year from now, we will be able to claim substantial progress toward both those objectives.

End Notes

[1] Of course, these interventions were not the first of the crisis. For example, in July and August of 2007, two German banks that had relied heavily on market funding through asset-backed commercial paper (ABCP) conduits--IKB and Sachsen LB--received assistance from public-sector owners to cope with severe funding pressures. In September 2007, Northern Rock, a large mortgage lender that relied heavily on securitizations for funding, was nationalized by U.K. authorities after experiencing a run by retail depositors. In February 2008, West LB--another German bank with large ABCP conduits--received protection against losses from its owners, including the state of North Rhine-Westphalia. And in March 2008, the U.S. Treasury and the Federal Reserve facilitated the acquisition of the investment bank Bear Stearns by JPMorgan Chase & Co.

[2] Throughout these remarks, where examples are given, they represent only a selection of instances, not an exhaustive list of all the relevant cases.

[3] Prime money funds hold a variety of instruments, with commercial paper and bank obligations typically accounting for the majority of their assets.

[4] For example, most financing of automobile purchases was provided through nonbank channels, and such channels began shutting down in September and October of 2008.

[5] More precisely, in the Commercial Paper Funding Facility (CPFF), the Fed lends to a special purpose vehicle that, in turn, purchases highly rated three-month commercial paper directly from eligible issuers. On October 21, the Fed also announced the creation of the Money Market Investor Funding Facility, or MMIFF, which was intended to provide a source of backup liquidity to U.S. money market mutual funds and certain other money market investors. Given the improvement in short-term markets brought about by the Asset-Backed Commercial Paper Money Market Mutual Fund Liquidity Facility (AMLF), the CPFF, and

the Treasury guarantee of money market funds, the MMIFF never had to be tapped. Nonetheless, market participants reported that the facility's existence helped reassure investors that ample liquidity would be available in case of further disruptions in the money markets.

[6] A crucial feature of these lines is that the Federal Reserve's counterparties are the foreign central banks, which are governmental entities, not the private-sector entities to which those central banks might lend in turn. Accordingly, the Fed bears little risk through these arrangements.

[7] Notably, these commitments were reaffirmed on October 11 in communiqués issued by the International Monetary and Financial Committee of the Board of Governors of the IMF and by the Group of Twenty finance ministers and central bank governors.

[8] The FDIC's guarantee program complemented a temporary increase in the deposit insurance limit, from $100,000 to $250,000 per account, passed by the Congress as part of the Emergency Economic Stabilization Act, the bill that created the TARP.

[9] On January 26, the Dutch government announced that it would provide ING Group, a large banking and insurance firm, with loss protection on some of its assets, following up a €10 billion capital injection on October 19. Shortly afterward, the U.K. Treasury announced packages for the Royal Bank of Scotland (RBS) and for Lloyds Banking Group that included loss protection on assets and, in the case of RBS, a capital injection.

[10] In March, the Federal Reserve announced that it would purchase up to $300 billion of longer-term Treasury securities and raised the caps on other purchases to $200 billion for the direct debt of the housing-related GSEs and $1.25 trillion for agency-guaranteed mortgage-backed securities.

[11] Officially, it was called the Supervisory Capital Assessment Program, or SCAP.

[12] See Walter Bagehot ([1873] 1897), *Lombard Street: A Description of the Money Market* (New York: Charles Scribner's Sons).

[13] The Northern Rock episode in the United Kingdom may be seen as a counterexample, but in that case deposit insurance coverage was only partial.

[14] To be sure, there are good economic reasons for a maturity mismatch between assets and liabilities in the financial system, including allowing households flexibility in when to consume (see Douglas W. Diamond and Philip H. Dybvig (1983), "Bank Runs, Deposit Insurance, and Liquidity," *Journal of Political Economy*, vol. 91 (June), pp. 401-19). Moreover, short-term creditors can help to impose market discipline on financial institutions (see Charles W. Calomiris and Charles M. Kahn (1991), "The Role of Demandable Debt in Structuring Optimal Banking Arrangements," *American Economic Review*, vol. 81 (June), pp. 497-513; and Douglas W. Diamond and Raghuram G. Rajan (2001), "Liquidity Risk, Liquidity Creation, and Financial Fragility: A Theory of Banking," *Journal of Political Economy*, vol. 109 (April), pp. 287-327).

[15] Also, during a panic, financial firms concerned about funding are likely to hoard liquidity, further exacerbating the situation. See Douglas W. Diamond and Raghuram G. Rajan (2009), "Fear of Fire Sales and the Credit Freeze," NBER Working Paper Series 14925 (Cambridge, Mass.: National Bureau of Economic Research, April); and Zhiguo He and Wei Xiong (2009), "Dynamic Debt Runs," unpublished paper, June 30, Princeton University, Princeton, N.J.

[16] See Markus K. Brunnermeier (2009), "Deciphering the Liquidity and Credit Crunch 2007-2008," *Journal of Economic Perspectives*, vol. 23 (Winter), pp. 77-100. This dynamic differed from the standard bank run in that investors did not completely withdraw funding. The reason for the difference lies in the nature of the lending contract. In a standard bank deposit contract, the price of deposits in terms of currency is fixed, and so depositors have no alternative to withdrawal when the value of deposits falls below the value of currency. For similar reasons, many investors in money market mutual funds withdrew all their funds when the redemption value exceeded the value of holding the fund. In contrast, in the case of repo lending, lenders have the alternative to withdrawal of varying the haircut they

demand. There is a close analogy to the discounting of bank notes during the U.S. free banking era, as discussed by Gorton (see Gary Gorton (1996), "Reputation Formation in Early Bank Note Markets," *Journal of Political Economy*, vol. 104 (April), pp. 346-97). In either case, however, variations in the liquidity premium play an important role in the amount of funding that lenders are willing to provide against a given set of assets.

[17] See Gary B. Gorton and Andrew Metrick (2009), "Securitized Banking and the Run on Repo," Yale International Center for Finance Working Paper No. 14, July.

[18] See Daniel M. Covitz, Nellie Liang, and Gustavo Suarez (2009), "The Evolution of a Financial Crisis: Runs in the Asset-Backed Commercial Paper Market," unpublished paper, Board of Governors of the Federal Reserve System, Division of Research and Statistics, August. Moreover, the scale of these conduits and their vulnerability to runs contributed importantly to the liquidity panics globally as many of these programs were sponsored by non-U.S. banks (see Carlos O. Arteta, Mark Carey, Ricardo Correa, and Jason Kotter (2009), "Revenge of the Steamroller: ABCP as a Window on Risk Choices," unpublished paper, Board of Governors of the Federal Reserve System, Division of International Finance, May).

[19] See Brian F. Madigan (2009), "Bagehot's Dictum in Practice: Formulating and Implementing Policies to Combat the Financial Crisis," speech delivered at this symposium, sponsored by the Federal Reserve Bank of Kansas City, Jackson Hole, Wyo., August 21-23.

[20] See Bagehot, *Lombard Street*.

[21] See Ben S. Bernanke (2009), "Financial Reform," speech delivered at the Council on Foreign Relations, Washington, March 10.

In: Bernanke and Greenspan
Editors R. Anderson, et al.
ISBN: 978-1-62100- 912-2

Chapter 4

AT THE FEDERAL RESERVE BANK OF KANSAS CITY'S ANNUAL ECONOMIC SYMPOSIUM, JACKSON HOLE, WYOMING AUGUST 22, 2008

Ben S. Bernanke

REDUCING SYSTEMIC RISK

In choosing the topic for this year's symposium--maintaining stability in a changing financial system--the Federal Reserve Bank of Kansas City staff is, once again, right on target. Although we have seen improved functioning in some markets, the financial storm that reached gale force some weeks before our last meeting here in Jackson Hole has not yet subsided, and its effects on the broader economy are becoming apparent in the form of softening economic activity and rising unemployment. Add to this mix a jump in inflation, in part the product of a global commodity boom, and the result has been one of the most challenging economic and policy environments in memory.

The Federal Reserve's response to this crisis has consisted of three key elements. First, we eased monetary policy substantially, particularly after indications of economic weakness proliferated around the turn of the year. In easing rapidly and proactively, we sought to offset, at least in part, the tightening of credit conditions associated with the crisis and thus to mitigate

Cthe effects on the broader economy. By cushioning the first-round economic impact of the financial stress, we hoped also to minimize the risks of a so-called adverse feedback loop in which economic weakness exacerbates financial stress, which, in turn, further damages economic prospects.

In view of the weakening outlook and the downside risks to growth, the Federal Open Market Committee (FOMC) has maintained a relatively low target for the federal funds rate despite an increase in inflationary pressures. This strategy has been conditioned on our expectation that the prices of oil and other commodities would ultimately stabilize, in part as the result of slowing global growth, and that this outcome, together with well-anchored inflation expectations and increased slack in resource utilization, would foster a return to price stability in the medium run. In this regard, the recent decline in commodity prices, as well as the increased stability of the dollar, has been encouraging. If not reversed, these developments, together with a pace of growth that is likely to fall short of potential for a time, should lead inflation to moderate later this year and next year. Nevertheless, the inflation outlook remains highly uncertain, not least because of the difficulty of predicting the future course of commodity prices, and we will continue to monitor inflation and inflation expectations closely. The FOMC is committed to achieving medium-term price stability and will act as necessary to attain that objective.

The second element of our response has been to offer liquidity support to the financial markets through a variety of collateralized lending programs. I have discussed these lending facilities and their rationale in some detail on other occasions.[1] Briefly, these programs are intended to mitigate what have been, at times, very severe strains in short-term funding markets and, by providing an additional source of financing, to allow banks and other financial institutions to deleverage in a more orderly manner. We have recently extended our special programs for primary dealers beyond the end of the year, based on our assessment that financial conditions remain unusual and exigent. We will continue to review all of our liquidity facilities to determine if they are having their intended effects or require modification.

The third element of our strategy encompasses a range of activities and initiatives undertaken in our role as financial regulator and supervisor, some of which I will describe in more detail later in my remarks. Briefly, these activities include cooperating with other regulators to monitor the health of individual financial institutions; working with the private sector to reduce risks in some key markets; developing new regulations, including new rules to govern mortgage and credit card lending; taking an active part in domestic and international efforts to draw out the lessons of the recent experience; and applying those lessons in our supervisory practices.

Closely related to this third group of activities is a critical question that we as a country now face: how to strengthen our financial system, including our system of financial regulation and supervision, to reduce the frequency and severity of bouts of financial instability in the future. In this regard, some particularly thorny issues are raised by the existence of financial institutions that may be perceived as "too big to fail" and the moral hazard issues that may arise when governments intervene in a financial crisis. As you know, in March the Federal Reserve acted to prevent the default of the investment bank Bear Stearns. For reasons that I will discuss shortly, those actions were necessary and justified under the circumstances that prevailed at that time. However, those events also have consequences that must be addressed. In particular, if no countervailing actions are taken, what would be perceived as an implicit expansion of the safety net could exacerbate the problem of "too big to fail," possibly resulting in excessive risk-taking and yet greater systemic risk in the future. Mitigating that problem is one of the design challenges that we face as we consider the future evolution of our system.

As both the nation's central bank and a financial regulator, the Federal Reserve must be well prepared to make constructive contributions to the coming national debate on the future of the financial system and financial regulation. Accordingly, we have set up a number of internal working groups, consisting of governors, Reserve Bank presidents, and staff, to study these and related issues. That work is ongoing, and I do not want to prejudge the outcomes. However, in the remainder of my remarks today I will raise, in a preliminary way, what I see as some promising approaches for reducing systemic risk. I will begin by discussing steps that are already under way to strengthen the financial infrastructure in a manner that should increase the resilience of our financial system. I will then turn to a discussion of regulatory and supervisory practice, with particular attention to whether a more comprehensive, systemwide perspective in financial supervision is warranted. For the most part, I will leave for another occasion the issues of broader structural and statutory change, such as those raised by the Treasury's blueprint for regulatory reform.[2]

Strengthening the Financial Infrastructure

An effective means of increasing the resilience of the financial system is to strengthen its infrastructure. For my purposes today, I want to construe "financial infrastructure" very broadly, to include not only the "hardware" components of that infrastructure--the physical systems on which market participants rely for the quick and accurate execution, clearing, and settlement of transactions--but also the associated "software," including the statutory, regulatory, and contractual frameworks and the business practices that govern the actions and obligations of market participants on both sides of each transaction. Of course, a robust financial infrastructure has many benefits even in normal times, including lower transactions costs and greater market liquidity. In periods of extreme stress, however, the quality of the financial infrastructure may prove critical. For example, it greatly affects the ability of market participants to quickly determine their own positions and exposures, including exposures to key counterparties, and to adjust their positions as necessary. When positions and exposures cannot be determined rapidly--as was the case, for example, when program trades overwhelmed the system during the 1987 stock market crash--potential outcomes include highly risk-averse behavior by market participants, sharp declines in market liquidity, and high volatility in asset prices. The financial infrastructure also has important effects on how market participants respond to perceived changes in counterparty risk. For example, during a period of heightened stress, participants may be willing to provide liquidity to a market if a strong central counterparty is present but not otherwise.

Considerations of this type were very much in our minds during the Bear Stearns episode in March. The collapse of Bear Stearns was triggered by a run of its creditors and customers, analogous to the run of depositors on a commercial bank. This run was surprising, however, in that Bear Stearns's borrowings were largely secured--that is, its lenders held collateral to ensure repayment even if the company itself failed. However, the illiquidity of markets in mid-March was so severe that creditors lost confidence that they could recoup their loans by selling the collateral. Many short-term lenders declined to renew their loans, driving Bear to the brink of default.

Although not an extraordinarily large company by many metrics, Bear Stearns was deeply involved in a number of critical markets, including (as I have noted) markets for short-term secured funding as well as those for over-the-counter (OTC) derivatives. One of our concerns was that the infrastructures of those markets and the risk- and liquidity-management practices of market participants would not be adequate to deal in an orderly way with the collapse of a major counterparty. With financial conditions already quite fragile, the sudden, unanticipated failure of Bear Stearns would have led to a sharp unwinding of positions in those markets that could have severely shaken the confidence of market participants. The company's failure could also have cast doubt on the financial conditions of some of Bear Stearns's many counterparties or of companies with similar businesses and funding practices, impairing the ability of those firms to meet their funding needs or to carry out normal transactions. As more firms lost access to funding, the vicious circle of forced selling, increased volatility, and higher haircuts and margin calls that was already well advanced at the time would likely have intensified. The broader economy could hardly have remained immune from such severe financial disruptions. Largely because of these concerns, the Federal Reserve took actions that facilitated the purchase of Bear Stearns and the assumption of Bear's financial obligations by JPMorgan Chase & Co.

This experience has led me to believe that one of the best ways to protect the financial system against future systemic shocks, including the possible failure of a major counterparty, is by strengthening the financial infrastructure, including both the "hardware" and the "software" components. The Federal Reserve, in collaboration with the private sector and other regulators, is intensively engaged in such efforts. For example, since September 2005, the Federal Reserve Bank of New York has been leading a joint public-private initiative to improve arrangements for clearing and settling trades in credit default swaps and other OTC derivatives. These efforts include gaining commitments from private-sector participants to automate and standardize the clearing and settlement process, encouraging improved netting and cash settlement arrangements, and supporting the development of a central counterparty for credit default swaps. More generally, although customized derivatives contracts between sophisticated counterparties will continue to be appropriate in many situations, on the margin it appears that a migration of derivatives trading toward more-standardized instruments and the increased use of well-managed central counterparties, either linked to or independent of exchanges, could have a systemic benefit.

The Federal Reserve and other authorities also are focusing on enhancing the resilience of the markets for triparty repurchase agreements (repos). In the triparty repo market, primary dealers and other large banks and broker-dealers obtain very large amounts of secured financing from money funds and other short-term, risk-averse investors. We are encouraging firms to improve their management of liquidity risk and to reduce over time their reliance on triparty repos for overnight financing of less-liquid forms of collateral. In the longer term, we need to ensure that there are robust contingency plans for managing, in an orderly manner, the default of a major participant. We should also explore possible means of reducing this market's dependence on large amounts of intraday credit from the banks that facilitate the settlement of triparty repos. The attainment of these objectives might be facilitated by the introduction of a central counterparty but may also be achievable under the current framework for clearing and settlement.

Of course, like other central banks, the Federal Reserve continues to monitor systemically important payment and settlement systems and to compare their performance with international standards for reliability, efficiency, and safety. Unlike most other central banks, however, the Federal Reserve does not have general statutory authority to oversee these systems. Instead, we rely on a patchwork of authorities, largely derived from our role as a banking supervisor, as well as on moral suasion, to help ensure that the various payment and settlement systems have the necessary procedures and controls in place to manage the risks they face. As part of any larger reform, the Congress should consider granting the Federal Reserve explicit oversight authority for systemically important payment and settlement systems.

Yet another key component of the software of the financial infrastructure is the set of rules and procedures used to resolve claims on a market participant that has defaulted on its obligations. In the overwhelming majority of cases, the bankruptcy laws and contractual agreements serve this function well. However, in the rare circumstances in which the impending or actual failure of an institution imposes substantial systemic risks, the standard procedures for resolving institutions may be inadequate. In the Bear Stearns case, the government's response was severely complicated by the lack of a clear statutory framework for dealing with such a situation. As I have suggested on other occasions, the Congress may wish to consider whether such a framework should be set up for a defined set of nonbank institutions.[3] A possible approach would be to give an agency--the Treasury seems an appropriate choice--the responsibility and the resources, under carefully specified conditions and in consultation with the appropriate supervisors, to intervene in cases in which an impending default by a major nonbank financial institution is judged to carry significant systemic risks. The implementation of such a resolution scheme does raise a number of complex issues, however, and further study will be needed to develop specific, workable proposals.

A stronger infrastructure would help to reduce systemic risk. Importantly, as my FOMC colleague Gary Stern has pointed out, it would also mitigate moral hazard and the problem of "too big to fail" by reducing the range of circumstances in which systemic stability concerns might be expected by markets to prompt government intervention.[4] A statutory resolution regime for nonbanks, besides reducing uncertainty, would also limit moral hazard by allowing the government to resolve failing firms in a way that is orderly but also wipes out equity holders and haircuts some creditors, analogous to what happens when a commercial bank fails.

A Systemwide Approach to Supervisory Oversight

The regulation and supervisory oversight of financial institutions is another critical tool for limiting systemic risk. In general, effective government oversight of individual institutions increases financial resilience and reduces moral hazard by attempting to ensure that all financial firms with access to some sort of federal safety net--including those that creditors may believe are too big to fail--maintain adequate buffers of capital and liquidity and develop comprehensive approaches to risk and liquidity management. Importantly, a well-designed supervisory regime complements rather than supplants market discipline. Indeed, regulation can serve to strengthen market discipline, for example, by mandating a transparent disclosure regime for financial firms.

Going forward, a critical question for regulators and supervisors is what their appropriate "field of vision" should be. Under our current system of safety-and-soundness regulation, supervisors often focus on the financial conditions of individual institutions in isolation. An alternative approach, which has been called systemwide or macroprudential oversight, would broaden the mandate of regulators and supervisors to encompass consideration of potential systemic risks and weaknesses as well.

At least informally, financial regulation and supervision in the United States already include some macroprudential elements. As one illustration, many of the supervisory guidances issued by federal bank regulators have been motivated, at least in part, by concerns that a particular industry trend posed risks to the stability of the banking system as a whole, not just to individual institutions. For example, following lengthy comment periods, in 2006, the federal banking supervisors issued formal guidance on underwriting and managing the risks of nontraditional mortgages, such as interest-only and negative amortization mortgages, as well as guidance warning banks against excessive concentrations in commercial real estate lending. These guidances likely would not have been issued if the federal regulators had viewed the issues they addressed as being isolated to a few banks. The regulators were concerned not only about individual banks but also about the systemic risks associated with excessive *industry-wide* concentrations (of commercial real estate or nontraditional mortgages) or an *industry-wide* pattern of certain practices (for example, in underwriting exotic mortgages). Note that, in warning against excessive concentrations or common exposures across the banking system, regulators need not make a judgment about whether a particular asset class is mispriced--although rapid changes in asset prices or risk premiums may increase the level of concern. Rather, their task is to determine the risks imposed on the system as a whole if common exposures significantly increase the correlation of returns across institutions.

The development of supervisory guidances is a process which often involves soliciting comments from the industry and the public and, where applicable, developing a consensus among the banking regulators. In that respect, the process is not always as nimble as we might like. For that reason, less-formal processes may sometimes be more effective and timely. As a case in point, the Federal Reserve--in close cooperation with other domestic and foreign regulators--regularly conducts so-called horizontal reviews of large financial institutions, focused on specific issues and practices. Recent reviews have considered topics such as leveraged loans, enterprise-wide risk management, and liquidity practices. The lessons learned from these reviews are shared with both the institutions participating in these reviews as well as other institutions for which the information might be beneficial. Like supervisory guidance, these reviews help increase the safety and soundness of individual institutions but they may also identify common weaknesses and risks that may have implications for broader systemic stability. In my view, making the systemic risk rationale for guidances and reviews more explicit is certainly feasible and would be a useful step toward a more systemic orientation for financial regulation and supervision.

A systemwide focus for financial regulation would also increase attention to how the incentives and constraints created by regulations affect behavior, especially risk-taking, through the credit cycle. During a period of economic weakness, for example, a prudential supervisor concerned only with the safety and soundness of a particular institution will tend to push for very conservative lending policies. In contrast, the macroprudential supervisor would recognize that, for the system as a whole, excessively conservative lending policies could prove counterproductive if they contribute to a weaker economic and credit environment. Similarly, risk concentrations that might be acceptable at a single institution in a period of economic expansion could be dangerous if they existed at a large number of institutions simultaneously. I do not have the time today to do justice to the question of the procyclicality of, say, capital regulations and accounting rules. This topic has received a great deal of attention elsewhere and has also engaged the attention of regulators; in particular, the framers of the Basel II capital accord have made significant efforts to measure regulatory capital needs "through the cycle" to mitigate procyclicality. However, as we consider ways to strengthen the system for the future in light of what we have learned over the past year, we should critically examine capital regulations, provisioning policies, and other rules applied to financial institutions to determine whether, collectively, they increase the procyclicality of credit extension beyond the point that is best for the system as a whole.

A yet more ambitious approach to macroprudential regulation would involve an attempt by regulators to develop a more fully integrated overview of the entire financial system. In principle, such an approach would appear well justified, as our financial system has become less bank-centered and because activities or risk-taking not permitted to regulated institutions have a way of migrating to other financial firms or markets. Some caution is in order, however, as this more comprehensive approach would be technically demanding and possibly very costly both for the regulators and the firms they supervise. It would likely require at least periodic surveillance and information-gathering from a wide range of nonbank institutions. Increased coordination would be required among the private- and public-sector supervisors of exchanges and other financial markets to keep up to date with evolving practices and products and to try to identify those which may pose risks outside the purview of each individual regulator. International regulatory coordination, already quite extensive, would need to be expanded further.

One might imagine also conducting formal stress tests, not at the firm level as occurs now, but for a range of firms and markets simultaneously. Doing so might reveal important interactions that are missed by stress tests at the level of the individual firm. For example, such an exercise might suggest that a sharp change in asset prices would not only affect the value of a particular firm's holdings but also impair liquidity in key markets, with adverse consequences for the ability of the firm to adjust its risk positions or obtain funding. Systemwide stress tests might also highlight common exposures and "crowded trades" that would not be visible in tests confined to one firm.

Again, however, we should not underestimate the technical and information requirements of conducting such exercises effectively. Financial markets move swiftly, firms' holdings and exposures change every day, and financial transactions do not respect national boundaries. Thus, the information requirements for conducting truly comprehensive macroprudential surveillance could be daunting indeed.

Macroprudential supervision also presents communication issues. For example, the expectations of the public and of financial market participants would have to be managed carefully, as such an approach would never eliminate financial crises entirely. Indeed, an expectation by financial market participants that financial crises will never occur would create its own form of moral hazard and encourage behavior that would make financial crises more, rather than less, likely.

With all these caveats, I believe that an increased focus on systemwide risks by regulators and supervisors is inevitable and desirable. However, as we proceed in that direction, we would be wise to maintain a realistic appreciation of the difficulties of comprehensive oversight in a financial system as large, diverse, and globalized as ours.

Conclusion

Although we at the Federal Reserve remain focused on addressing the current risks to economic and financial stability, we have also begun thinking about the lessons for the future. I have discussed today two strategies for reducing systemic risk: strengthening the financial infrastructure, broadly construed, and increasing the systemwide focus of financial regulation and supervision. Work on the financial infrastructure is already well under way, and I expect further progress as the public and private sectors cooperate to address common concerns. The adoption of a regulatory and supervisory approach with a heavier macroprudential focus has a strong rationale, but we should be careful about over-promising, as we are still rather far from having the capacity to implement such an approach in a thoroughgoing way. The Federal Reserve will continue to work with the Congress, other regulators, and the private sector to explore this and other strategies to increase financial stability.

When we last met here in Jackson Hole, the nature of the financial crisis and its implications for the economy were just coming into view. A year later, many challenges remain. I look forward to the insights into this experience that will be provided by the papers at this conference.

End Notes

[1] See, for example, Ben S. Bernanke (2008), "*Liquidity Provision by the Federal Reserve*," speech delivered (via satellite) at the Federal Reserve Bank of Atlanta Financial Markets Conference, Sea Island, Ga., May 13.

[2] See Department of the Treasury (March 2008), *Blueprint for a Modernized Financial Regulatory Structure*.

[3] Ben S. Bernanke (2008), "*Financial Regulation and Financial Stability*," speech delivered at the Federal Deposit Insurance Corporation's Forum on Mortgage Lending for Low and Moderate Income Households, Arlington, Va., July 8.

[4] See, for example, Gary H. Stern and Ron J. Feldman (2004), *Too Big to Fail: The Hazards of Bank Bailouts* (Washington: Brookings Institution Press).

In: Bernanke and Greenspan
Editors R. Anderson, et al.
ISBN: 978-1-62100- 912-2

Chapter 5

AT THE FEDERAL RESERVE BANK OF KANSAS CITY'S ECONOMIC SYMPOSIUM, JACKSON HOLE, WYOMING, AUGUST 31, 2007

Ben S. Bernanke

HOUSING, HOUSING FINANCE, AND MONETARY POLICY

Over the years, Tom Hoenig and his colleagues at the Federal Reserve Bank of Kansas City have done an excellent job of selecting interesting and relevant topics for this annual symposium. I think I can safely say that this year they have outdone themselves. Recently, the subject of housing finance has preoccupied financial-market participants and observers in the United States and around the world. The financial turbulence we have seen had its immediate origins in the problems in the subprime mortgage market, but the effects have been felt in the broader mortgage market and in financial markets more generally, with potential consequences for the performance of the overall economy.

In my remarks this morning, I will begin with some observations about recent market developments and their economic implications. I will then try to place recent events in a broader historical context by discussing the evolution of housing markets and housing finance in the United States. In particular, I will argue that, over the years, institutional changes in U.S. housing and mortgage markets have significantly influenced both the transmission of monetary policy and the economy's cyclical dynamics. As our system of housing finance continues to evolve, understanding these linkages not only provides useful insights into the past but also holds the promise of helping us better cope with the implications of future developments.

Recent Developments in Financial Markets and the Economy

I will begin my review of recent developments by discussing the housing situation. As you know, the downturn in the housing market, which began in the summer of 2005, has been sharp. Sales of new and existing homes have declined significantly from their mid-2005 peaks and have remained slow in recent months. As demand has weakened, house prices have decelerated or even declined by some measures, and homebuilders have scaled back their construction of new homes. The cutback in residential construction has directly reduced the annual rate of U.S. economic growth about 3/4 percentage point on average over the past year and a half. Despite the slowdown in construction, the stock of unsold new homes remains quite elevated relative to sales, suggesting that further declines in homebuilding are likely.

The outlook for home sales and construction will also depend on unfolding developments in mortgage markets. A substantial increase in lending to nonprime borrowers contributed to the bulge in residential investment in 2004 and 2005, and the tightening of credit conditions for these borrowers likely accounts for some of the continued softening in demand we have seen this year. As I will discuss, recent market developments have resulted in additional tightening of rates and terms for nonprime borrowers as well as for potential borrowers through "jumbo" mortgages. Obviously, if current conditions persist in mortgage markets, the demand for homes could weaken further, with possible implications for the broader economy. We are following these developments closely.

As house prices have softened, and as interest rates have risen from the low levels of a couple of years ago, we have seen a marked deterioration in the performance of nonprime mortgages. The problems have been most severe for subprime mortgages with adjustable rates: the proportion of those loans with serious delinquencies rose to about 13-1/2 percent in June, more than double the recent low seen in mid-2005.[1] The adjustable-rate subprime mortgages originated in late 2005 and in 2006 have performed the worst, in part because of slippage in underwriting standards, reflected for example in high loan-to-value ratios and incomplete documentation. With many of these borrowers facing their first interest rate resets in coming quarters, and with softness in house prices expected to continue to impede refinancing, delinquencies among this class of mortgages are likely to rise further. Apart from adjustable-rate subprime mortgages, however, the deterioration in performance has been less pronounced, at least to this point. For subprime mortgages with fixed rather than variable rates, for example, serious delinquencies have been fairly stable at about 5-1/2 percent. The rate of serious delinquencies on alt-A securitized pools rose to nearly 3 percent in June, from a low of less than 1 percent in mid-2005. Delinquency rates on prime jumbo mortgages have also risen, though they are lower than those for prime conforming loans, and both rates are below 1 percent.

Investors' concerns about mortgage credit performance have intensified sharply in recent weeks, reflecting, among other factors, worries about the housing market and the effects of impending interest-rate resets on borrowers' ability to remain current. Credit spreads on new securities backed by subprime mortgages, which had jumped earlier this year, rose significantly more in July. Issuance of such securities has been negligible since then, as dealers have faced difficulties placing even the AAA-rated tranches. Issuance of securities backed by alt-A and prime jumbo mortgages also has fallen sharply, as investors have evidently become concerned that the losses associated with these types of mortgages may be higher than had been expected.

With securitization impaired, some major lenders have announced the cancellation of their adjustable-rate subprime lending programs. A number of others that specialize in nontraditional mortgages have been forced by funding pressures to scale back or close down. Some lenders that sponsor asset-backed commercial paper conduits as bridge financing for their mortgage originations have been unable to "roll" the maturing paper, forcing them to draw on back-up liquidity facilities or to exercise options to extend the maturity of their paper. As a result of these developments, borrowers face noticeably tighter terms and standards for all but conforming mortgages.

As you know, the financial stress has not been confined to mortgage markets. The markets for asset-backed commercial paper and for lower-rated unsecured commercial paper market also have suffered from pronounced declines in investor demand, and the associated flight to quality has contributed to surges in the demand for short-dated Treasury bills, pushing T-bill rates down sharply on some days. Swings in stock prices have been sharp, with implied price volatilities rising to about twice the levels seen in the spring. Credit spreads for a range of financial instruments have widened, notably for lower-rated corporate credits. Diminished demand for loans and bonds to finance highly leveraged transactions has increased some banks' concerns that they may have to bring significant quantities of these instruments onto their balance sheets. These banks, as well as those that have committed to serve as back-up facilities to commercial paper programs, have become more protective of their liquidity and balance-sheet capacity.

Although this episode appears to have been triggered largely by heightened concerns about subprime mortgages, global financial losses have far exceeded even the most pessimistic projections of credit losses on those loans. In part, these wider losses likely reflect concerns that weakness in U.S. housing will restrain overall economic growth. But other factors are also at work. Investor uncertainty has increased significantly, as the difficulty of evaluating the risks of structured products that can be opaque or have complex payoffs has become more evident. Also, as in many episodes of financial stress, uncertainty about possible forced sales by leveraged participants and a higher cost of risk capital seem to have made investors hesitant to take advantage of possible buying opportunities. More generally, investors may have become less willing to assume risk. Some increase in the premiums that investors require to take risk is probably a healthy development on the whole, as these premiums have been exceptionally low for some time. However, in this episode, the shift in risk attitudes has interacted with heightened concerns about credit risks and uncertainty about how to evaluate those risks to create significant market stress. On the positive side of the ledger, we should recognize that past efforts to strengthen capital positions and the financial infrastructure place the global financial system in a relatively strong position to work through this process.

In the statement following its August 7 meeting, the Federal Open Market Committee (FOMC) recognized that the rise in financial volatility and the tightening of credit conditions for some households and businesses had increased the downside risks to growth somewhat but reiterated that inflation risks remained its predominant policy concern. In subsequent days, however, following several events that led investors to believe that credit risks might be larger and more pervasive than previously thought, the functioning of financial markets became increasingly impaired. Liquidity dried up and spreads widened as many market participants sought to retreat from certain types of asset exposures altogether.

Well-functioning financial markets are essential for a prosperous economy. As the nation's central bank, the Federal Reserve seeks to promote general financial stability and to help to ensure that financial markets function in an orderly manner. In response to the developments in the financial markets in the period following the FOMC meeting, the Federal Reserve provided reserves to address unusual strains in money markets. On August 17, the Federal Reserve Board announced a cut in the discount rate of 50 basis points and adjustments in the Reserve Banks' usual discount window practices to facilitate the provision of term financing for as long as thirty days, renewable by the borrower. The Federal Reserve also took a number of supplemental actions, such as cutting the fee charged for lending Treasury securities. The purpose of the discount window actions was to assure depositories of the ready availability of a backstop source of liquidity. Even if banks find that borrowing from the discount window is not immediately necessary, the knowledge that liquidity is available should help alleviate concerns about funding that might otherwise constrain depositories from extending credit or making markets. The Federal Reserve stands ready to take additional actions as needed to provide liquidity and promote the orderly functioning of markets.

It is not the responsibility of the Federal Reserve--nor would it be appropriate--to protect lenders and investors from the consequences of their financial decisions. But developments in financial markets can have broad economic effects felt by many outside the markets, and the Federal Reserve must take those effects into account when determining policy. In a statement issued simultaneously with the discount window announcement, the FOMC indicated that the deterioration in financial market conditions and the tightening of credit since its August 7 meeting had appreciably increased the downside risks to growth. In particular, the further tightening of credit conditions, if sustained, would increase the risk that the current weakness in housing could be deeper or more prolonged than previously expected, with possible adverse effects on consumer spending and the economy more generally.

The incoming data indicate that the economy continued to expand at a moderate pace into the summer, despite the sharp correction in the housing sector. However, in light of recent financial developments, economic data bearing on past months or quarters may be less useful than usual for our forecasts of economic activity and inflation. Consequently, we will pay particularly close attention to the timeliest indicators, as well as information gleaned from our business and banking contacts around the country. Inevitably, the uncertainty surrounding the outlook will be greater than normal, presenting a challenge to policymakers to manage the risks to their growth and price stability objectives. The Committee continues to monitor the situation and will act as needed to limit the adverse effects on the broader economy that may arise from the disruptions in financial markets.

Beginnings: Mortgage Markets in the Early Twentieth Century

Like us, our predecessors grappled with the economic and policy implications of innovations and institutional changes in housing finance. In the remainder of my remarks, I will try to set the stage for this weekend's conference by discussing the historical evolution of the mortgage market and some of the implications of that evolution for monetary policy and the economy.

The early decades of the twentieth century are a good starting point for this review, as urbanization and the exceptionally rapid population growth of that period created a strong demand for new housing. Between 1890 and 1930, the number of housing units in the United States grew from about 10 million to about 30 million; the pace of homebuilding was particularly brisk during the economic boom of the 1920s.

Remarkably, this rapid expansion of the housing stock took place despite limited sources of mortgage financing and typical lending terms that were far less attractive than those to which we are accustomed today. Required down payments, usually about half of the home's purchase price, excluded many households from the market. Also, by comparison with today's standards, the duration of mortgage loans was short, usually ten years or less. A "balloon" payment at the end of the loan often created problems for borrowers.[2]

High interest rates on loans reflected the illiquidity and the essentially unhedgeable interest rate risk and default risk associated with mortgages. Nationwide, the average spread between mortgage rates and high-grade corporate bond yields during the 1920s was about 200 basis points, compared with about 50 basis points on average since the mid-1980s. The absence of a national capital market also produced significant regional disparities in borrowing costs. Hard as it may be to conceive today, rates on mortgage loans before World War I were at times as much as 2 to 4 percentage points higher in some parts of the country than in others, and even in 1930, regional differences in rates could be more than a full percentage point.[3]

Despite the underdevelopment of the mortgage market, homeownership rates rose steadily after the turn of the century. As would often be the case in the future, government policy provided some inducement for homebuilding. When the federal income tax was introduced in 1913, it included an exemption for mortgage interest payments, a provision that is a powerful stimulus to housing demand even today. By 1930, about 46 percent of nonfarm households owned their own homes, up from about 37 percent in 1890.

The limited availability of data prior to 1929 makes it hard to quantify the role of housing in the monetary policy transmission mechanism during the early twentieth century. Comparisons are also complicated by great differences between then and now in monetary policy frameworks and tools. Still, then as now, periods of tight money were reflected in higher interest rates and a greater reluctance of banks to lend, which affected conditions in mortgage markets. Moreover, students of the business cycle, such as Arthur Burns and Wesley Mitchell, have observed that residential construction was highly cyclical and contributed significantly to fluctuations in the overall economy (Burns and Mitchell, 1946). Indeed, if we take the somewhat less reliable data for 1901 to 1929 at face value, real housing investment was about three times as volatile during that era as it has been over the past half-century.

During the past century we have seen two great sea changes in the market for housing finance. The first of these was the product of the New Deal. The second arose from financial innovation and a series of crises from the 1960s to the mid-1980s in depository funding of mortgages. I will turn first to the New Deal period.

The New Deal and the Housing Market

The housing sector, like the rest of the economy, was profoundly affected by the Great Depression. When Franklin Roosevelt took office in 1933, almost 10 percent of all homes were in foreclosure (Green and Wachter, 2005), construction employment had fallen by half from its late 1920s peak, and a banking system near collapse was providing little new credit. As in other sectors, New Deal reforms in housing and housing finance aimed to foster economic revival through government programs that either provided financing directly or strengthened the institutional and regulatory structure of private credit markets.

Actually, one of the first steps in this direction was taken not by Roosevelt but by his predecessor, Herbert Hoover, who oversaw the creation of the Federal Home Loan Banking System in 1932. This measure reorganized the thrift industry (savings and loans and mutual savings banks) under federally chartered associations and established a credit reserve system modeled after the Federal Reserve. The Roosevelt administration pushed this and other programs affecting housing finance much further. In 1934, his administration oversaw the creation of the Federal Housing Administration (FHA). By providing a federally backed insurance system for mortgage lenders, the FHA was designed to encourage lenders to offer mortgages on more attractive terms. This intervention appears to have worked in that, by the 1950s, most new mortgages were for thirty years at fixed rates, and down payment requirements had fallen to about 20 percent. In 1938, the Congress chartered the Federal National Mortgage Association, or Fannie Mae, as it came to be known. The new institution was authorized to issue bonds and use the proceeds to purchase FHA mortgages from lenders, with the objectives of increasing the supply of mortgage credit and reducing variations in the terms and supply of credit across regions.[4]

Shaped to a considerable extent by New Deal reforms and regulations, the postwar mortgage market took on the form that would last for several decades. The market had two main sectors. One, the descendant of the pre-Depression market sector, consisted of savings and loan associations, mutual savings banks, and, to a lesser extent, commercial banks. With financing from short-term deposits, these institutions made conventional fixed-rate long-term loans to homebuyers. Notably, federal and state regulations limited geographical diversification for these lenders, restricting interstate banking and obliging thrifts to make mortgage loans in small local areas--within 50 miles of the home office until 1964, and within 100 miles after that. In the other sector, the product of New Deal programs, private mortgage brokers and other lenders originated standardized loans backed by the FHA and the Veterans' Administration (VA). These guaranteed loans could be held in portfolio or sold to institutional investors through a nationwide secondary market.

No discussion of the New Deal's effect on the housing market and the monetary transmission mechanism would be complete without reference to Regulation Q--which was eventually to exemplify the law of unintended consequences. The Banking Acts of 1933 and 1935 gave the Federal Reserve the authority to impose deposit-rate ceilings on banks, an authority that was later expanded to cover thrift institutions. The Fed used this authority in establishing its Regulation Q. The so-called Reg Q ceilings remained in place in one form or another until the mid-1980s.[5]

The original rationale for deposit ceilings was to reduce "excessive" competition for bank deposits, which some blamed as a cause of bank failures in the early 1930s. In retrospect, of course, this was a dubious bit of economic analysis. In any case, the principal effects of the ceilings were not on bank competition but on the supply of credit. With the ceilings in place, banks and thrifts experienced what came to be known as disintermediation--an outflow of funds from depositories that occurred whenever short-term money-market rates rose above the maximum that these institutions could pay. In the absence of alternative funding sources, the loss of deposits prevented banks and thrifts from extending mortgage credit to new customers.

The Transmission Mechanism and the New Deal Reforms

Under the New Deal system, housing construction soared after World War II, driven by the removal of wartime building restrictions, the need to replace an aging housing stock, rapid family formation that accompanied the beginning of the baby boom, and large-scale internal migration. The stock of housing units grew 20 percent between 1940 and 1950, with most of the new construction occurring after 1945.

In 1951, the Treasury-Federal Reserve Accord freed the Fed from the obligation to support Treasury bond prices. Monetary policy began to focus on influencing short-term money markets as a means of affecting economic activity and inflation, foreshadowing the Federal Reserve's current use of the federal funds rate as a policy instrument. Over the next few decades, housing assumed a leading role in the monetary transmission mechanism, largely for two reasons: Reg Q and the advent of high inflation.

The Reg Q ceilings were seldom binding before the mid-1960s, but disintermediation induced by the ceilings occurred episodically from the mid-1960s until Reg Q began to be phased out aggressively in the early 1980s. The impact of disintermediation on the housing market could be quite significant; for example, a moderate tightening of monetary policy in 1966 contributed to a 23 percent decline in residential construction between the first quarter of 1966 and the first quarter of 1967. State usury laws and branching restrictions worsened the episodes of disintermediation by placing ceilings on lending rates and limiting the flow of funds between local markets. For the period 1960 to 1982, when Reg Q assumed its greatest importance, statistical analysis shows a high correlation between single-family housing starts and the growth of small time deposits at thrifts, suggesting that disintermediation effects were powerful; in contrast, since 1983 this correlation is essentially zero.[6]

Economists at the time were well aware of the importance of the disintermediation phenomenon for monetary policy. Frank de Leeuw and Edward Gramlich highlighted this particular channel in their description of an early version of the MPS macroeconometric model, a joint product of researchers at the Federal Reserve, MIT, and the University of Pennsylvania (de Leeuw and Gramlich, 1969). The model attributed almost one-half of the direct first-year effects of monetary policy on the real economy--which were estimated to be substantial--to disintermediation and other housing-related factors, despite the fact that residential construction accounted for only 4 percent of nominal gross domestic product (GDP) at the time.

As time went on, however, monetary policy mistakes and weaknesses in the structure of the mortgage market combined to create deeper economic problems. For reasons that have been much analyzed, in the late 1960s and the 1970s the Federal Reserve allowed inflation to rise, which led to corresponding increases in nominal interest rates. Increases in short-term nominal rates not matched by contractually set rates on existing mortgages exposed a fundamental weakness in the system of housing finance, namely, the maturity mismatch between long-term mortgage credit and the short-term deposits that commercial banks and thrifts used to finance mortgage lending. This mismatch led to a series of liquidity crises and, ultimately, to a rash of insolvencies among mortgage lenders. High inflation was also ultimately reflected in high nominal long-term rates on new mortgages, which had the effect of "front loading" the real payments made by holders of long-term, fixed-rate mortgages. This front-loading reduced affordability and further limited the extension of mortgage credit, thereby restraining construction activity. Reflecting these factors, housing construction experienced a series of pronounced boom and bust cycles from the early 1960s through the mid-1980s, which contributed in turn to substantial swings in overall economic growth.

The Emergence of Capital Markets as a Source of Housing Finance

The manifest problems associated with relying on short-term deposits to fund long-term mortgage lending set in train major changes in financial markets and financial instruments, which collectively served to link mortgage lending more closely to the broader capital markets. The shift from reliance on specialized portfolio lenders financed by deposits to a greater use of capital markets represented the second great sea change in mortgage finance, equaled in importance only by the events of the New Deal.

Government actions had considerable influence in shaping this second revolution. In 1968, Fannie Mae was split into two agencies: the Government National Mortgage Association (Ginnie Mae) and the re-chartered Fannie Mae, which became a privately owned government-sponsored enterprise (GSE), authorized to operate in the secondary market for conventional as well as guaranteed mortgage loans. In 1970, to compete with Fannie Mae in the secondary market, another GSE was created--the Federal Home Loan Mortgage Corporation, or Freddie Mac. Also in 1970, Ginnie Mae issued the first mortgage pass-through security, followed soon after by Freddie Mac. In the early 1980s, Freddie Mac introduced collateralized mortgage obligations (CMOs), which separated the payments from a pooled set of mortgages into "strips" carrying different effective maturities and credit risks. Since 1980, the outstanding volume of GSE mortgage-backed securities has risen from less than $200 billion to more than $4 trillion today. Alongside these developments came the establishment of private mortgage insurers, which competed with the FHA, and private mortgage pools, which bundled loans not handled by the GSEs, including loans that did not meet GSE eligibility criteria--so-called nonconforming loans. Today, these private pools account for around $2 trillion in residential mortgage debt.

These developments did not occur in time to prevent a large fraction of the thrift industry from becoming effectively insolvent by the early 1980s in the wake of the late-1970s surge in inflation.[7] In this instance, the government abandoned attempts to patch up the system and instead undertook sweeping deregulation. Reg Q was phased out during the 1980s; state usury laws capping mortgage rates were abolished; restrictions on interstate banking were lifted by the mid-1990s; and lenders were permitted to offer adjustable-rate mortgages as well as mortgages that did not fully amortize and which therefore involved balloon payments at the end of the loan period. Critically, the savings and loan crisis of the late 1980s ended the dominance of deposit-taking portfolio lenders in the mortgage market. By the 1990s, increased reliance on securitization led to a greater separation between mortgage lending and mortgage investing even as the mortgage and capital markets became more closely integrated. About 56 percent of the home mortgage market is now securitized, compared with only 10 percent in 1980 and less than 1 percent in 1970.

In some ways, the new mortgage market came to look more like a textbook financial market, with fewer institutional "frictions" to impede trading and pricing of event-contingent securities. Securitization and the development of deep and liquid derivatives markets eased the spreading and trading of risk. New types of mortgage products were created. Recent developments notwithstanding, mortgages became more liquid instruments, for both lenders and borrowers. Technological advances facilitated these changes; for example, computerization and innovations such as credit scores reduced the costs of making loans and led to a "commoditization" of mortgages. Access to mortgage credit also widened; notably, loans to subprime borrowers accounted for about 13 percent of outstanding mortgages in 2006.

I suggested that the mortgage market has become more like the frictionless financial market of the textbook, with fewer institutional or regulatory barriers to efficient operation. In one important respect, however, that characterization is not entirely accurate. A key function of efficient capital markets is to overcome problems of information and incentives in the extension of credit. The traditional model of mortgage markets, based on portfolio lending, solved these problems in a straightforward way: Because banks and thrifts kept the loans they made on their own books, they had strong incentives to underwrite carefully and to invest in gathering information about borrowers and communities. In contrast, when most loans are securitized and originators have little financial or reputational capital at risk, the danger exists that the originators of loans will be less diligent. In securitization markets, therefore, monitoring the originators and ensuring that they have incentives to make good loans is critical. I have argued elsewhere that, in some cases, the failure of investors to provide adequate oversight of originators and to ensure that originators' incentives were properly aligned was a major cause of the problems that we see today in the subprime mortgage market (Bernanke, 2007). In recent months we have seen a reassessment of the problems of maintaining adequate monitoring and incentives in the lending process, with investors insisting on tighter underwriting standards and some large lenders pulling back from the use of brokers and other agents. We will not return to the days in which all mortgage lending was portfolio lending, but clearly the originate-to-distribute model will be modified--is already being modified--to provide stronger protection for investors and better incentives for originators to underwrite prudently.

The Monetary Transmission Mechanism since the Mid-1980s

The dramatic changes in mortgage finance that I have described appear to have significantly affected the role of housing in the monetary transmission mechanism. Importantly, the easing of some traditional institutional and regulatory frictions seems to have reduced the sensitivity of residential construction to monetary policy, so that housing is no longer so central to monetary transmission as it was.[8] In particular, in the absence of Reg Q ceilings on deposit rates and with a much-reduced role for deposits as a source of housing finance, the availability of mortgage credit today is generally less dependent on conditions in short-term money markets, where the central bank operates most directly.

Most estimates suggest that, because of the reduced sensitivity of housing to short-term interest rates, the response of the economy to a given change in the federal funds rate is modestly smaller and more balanced across sectors than in the past.[9] These results are embodied in the Federal Reserve's large econometric model of the economy, which implies that only about 14 percent of the overall response of output to monetary policy is now attributable to movements in residential investment, in contrast to the model's estimate of 25 percent or so under what I have called the New Deal system.

The econometric findings seem consistent with the reduced synchronization of the housing cycle and the business cycle during the present decade. In all but one recession during the period from 1960 to 1999, declines in residential investment accounted for at least 40 percent of the decline in overall real GDP, and the sole exception--the 1970 recession--was preceded by a substantial decline in housing activity before the official start of the downturn. In contrast, residential investment *boosted* overall real GDP growth during the 2001 recession. More recently, the sharp slowdown in housing has been accompanied, at least thus far, by relatively good performance in other sectors. That said, the current episode demonstrates that pronounced housing cycles are not a thing of the past.

My discussion so far has focused primarily on the role of variations in housing finance and residential construction in monetary transmission. But, of course, housing may have indirect effects on economic activity, most notably by influencing consumer spending. With regard to household consumption, perhaps the most significant effect of recent developments in mortgage finance is that home equity, which was once a highly illiquid asset, has become instead quite liquid, the result of the development of home equity lines of credit and the relatively low cost of cash-out refinancing. Economic theory suggests that the greater liquidity of home equity should allow households to better smooth consumption over time. This smoothing in turn should reduce the dependence of their spending on current income, which, by limiting the power of conventional multiplier effects, should tend to increase macroeconomic stability and reduce the effects of a given change in the short-term interest rate. These inferences are supported by some empirical evidence.[10]

On the other hand, the increased liquidity of home equity may lead consumer spending to respond more than in past years to changes in the values of their homes; some evidence does suggest that the correlation of consumption and house prices is higher in countries, like the United States, that have more sophisticated mortgage markets (Calza, Monacelli, and Stracca, 2007). Whether the development of home equity loans and easier mortgage refinancing has increased the magnitude of the real estate wealth effect--and if so, by how much--is a much-debated question that I will leave to another occasion.

CONCLUSION

I hope this exploration of the history of housing finance has persuaded you that institutional factors can matter quite a bit in determining the influence of monetary policy on housing and the role of housing in the business cycle. Certainly, recent developments have added yet further evidence in support of that proposition. The interaction of housing, housing finance, and economic activity has for years been of central importance for understanding the behavior of the economy, and it will continue to be central to our thinking as we try to anticipate economic and financial developments.

In closing, I would like to express my particular appreciation for an individual whom I count as a friend, as I know many of you do: Edward Gramlich. Ned was scheduled to be on the program but his illness prevented him from making the trip. As many of you know, Ned has been a research leader in the topics we are discussing this weekend, and he has just finished a very interesting book on subprime mortgage markets. We will miss not only Ned's insights over the course of this conference but his warmth and wit as well. Ned and his wife Ruth will be in the thoughts of all of us.

REFERENCES

[1] Benito, A., Thompson, J., Waldron, M. & R. Wood. (2006). *"House Bank of England Quarterly Bulletin*, vol. *46* (Summer), 142-54.

[2] Bennett, P., Peach, R. & Peristiani, S. (2001). "Structural Change in the

Mortgage Market and the Propensity to Refinance," *Journal of Money, Credit and Banking*, vol. *33* (no. 4), 955-75.

[3] Bernanke, Ben S. (2007). *"The Subprime Mortgage Market,"* speech delivered at the Federal Reserve Bank of Chicago's 43rd Annual Conference on Bank Structure and Competition, Chicago, May 17, www.federalreserve.gov/boarddocs/speeches/2007.

[4] Burns, Arthur F. & Wesley C. Mitchell. (1946). *Measuring Business Cycles* (New York: National Bureau of Economic Research).

[5] Calza, A., T. Monacelli & L. Stracca. (2007). *"Mortgage Markets, Collateral Constraints, and Monetary Policy: Do Institutional Factors Matter?"* CFS Working Paper Series No. 2007/10 (Frankfurt: Center for Financial Studies).

[6] de Leeuw, Frank & Edward M. Gramlich. (1969). *"The Channels of Monetary Policy: A Further Report on the Federal Reserve-MIT Model," Journal of Finance*, vol. *24* (May, Papers and Proceedings of the American Finance Association), 265-90.

[7] Dynan, Karen E., Douglas W. Elmendorf & Daniel E. Sichel. (2005). "Can Financial Innovation Help to Explain the Reduced Volatility of Economic Activity?" *Journal of Monetary Economics*, vol. *53* (January), 123-50.

[8] Estrella, Arturo. (2002). *"Securitization and the Efficacy of Monetary Policy"* Federal Reserve Bank of New York, *Economic Policy Review*, vol. *9* (May), 243-55.

[9] Green, Richard K. & Susan M. Wachter. (2005). *"The American Mortgage in Historical and International Context" Journal of Economic Perspectives*, vol. *19* (no. 4), 93-114.

[10] Hurst, E. & Stafford, F. (2004). *"Home is Where the Equity Is: Mortgage Refinancing and Household Consumption" Journal of Money, Credit and Banking*, vol. *36* (no. 6), 985-1014.

[11] Mahoney, Patrick I. & Alice P. White. (1985). "The Thrift Industry in Transition," *Federal Reserve Bulletin*, vol. *71* (March), 137-56.

[12] McCarthy, J. & Peach, R. (2002). *"Monetary Policy Transmission to Residential* Federal Reserve Bank of New York, *Economic Policy Review*, vol. *8* (no. 1), 139-58.

[13] Snowden, Kenneth A. (1987). "Mortgage Rates and American Capital Market Development in the Late Nineteenth Century," *Journal of Economic History*, vol. *47* (no. 3), 671-91.

[14] `U.S. Department of Commerce. (1937). *Financial Survey of Urban*

Housing (Washington: Government Printing Office).

[15] Weiss, Marc A. (1989). *"Marketing and Financing Home Ownership: Mortgage Lending and Public Policy in the United* in *Business and Economic History*, series 2, vol. *18*, William J. Hausman, ed., Wilmington, Del.: Business History Conference, 109-18.

End Notes

[1] Estimates of delinquencies are based on data from First American LoanPerformance.

[2] Weiss (1989) provides an overview of the evolution of mortgage lending over the past 100 years.

[3] Snowden (1987) discusses regional variations in home mortgage rates at the end of the nineteenth century. In addition, the U.S. Department of Commerce (1937) provides information on mortgage rates for various U.S. cities for the 1920s and early 1930s.

[4] Later, in anticipation of the end of World War II, the Congress created the Veterans' Administration Home Loan Guarantee Program, which supported mortgage lending to returning GIs on attractive terms, often including little or no down-payment requirement. In 1948, the Congress authorized Fannie Mae to purchase these VA loans as well.

[5] Regulation Q provisions that still exist restrict banks' ability to pay interest on some deposits, but these remaining provisions have little effect on the ability of depository institutions to raise funds.

[6] In detrended data, the correlation between quarterly single-family housing starts and the growth of small time deposits at thrifts during the preceding quarter was 0.53 for the 1960-1982 period; since 1983, this correlation has fallen to -0.02.

[7] Mahoney and White (1985) reported that the net worth of 156 thrift institutions was less than 1 percent of assets in 1984; when reported net worth was adjusted to exclude regulatory additions that did not represent true capital, this figure swelled to 253.

[8] Institutional factors can still be relevant, however, as can be seen by international comparisons. For example, in the United Kingdom, where the predominance of adjustable-rate mortgages makes changes in short-term interest rates quite visible to borrowers and homeowners, housing has a significant role in the monetary transmission mechanism through cash-flow effects on consumption, among other channels (Benito, Thompson, Waldron and Wood, 2006). Although adjustable-rate mortgages have become more important in the United States and now account for about 40 percent of the market, most adjustable-rate mortgages here are actually hybrids in that they bear a fixed rate for the first several years of the loan.

[9] For example, McCarthy and Peach (2002) report a substantial decline in the short-run, though not long-run, interest elasticity of residential investment and real GDP after the early 1980s. Work by Dynan, Elmendorf, and Sichel (2006) supports this conclusion as does other work at the Federal Reserve on models for forecasting residential investment. Modeling work at the Fed also shows that the short-run sensitivity of residential investment to nominal mortgage rates fell by more than half after the end of the New Deal system, but, in line with the findings of McCarthy and Peach, remained largely static after 1982. Estrella (2002) finds that secular changes in mortgage securitization have reduced the interest sensitivity of housing to short-term interest rates and the response of real output to an unanticipated change in monetary policy.

[10] Dynan, Elmendorf and Sichel (2006) argue that financial innovation has made it easier for households to use the equity in their homes to buffer their spending against income shocks, thereby reducing the volatility of aggregate consumption. Studies by Hurst and Stafford

(2004) and Bennett, Peach and Peristiani (2001) provide indirect evidence supporting this argument.

In: Bernanke and Greenspan
Editors R. Anderson, et al.
ISBN: 978-1-62100- 912-2

Chapter 6

AT THE FEDERAL RESERVE BANK OF KANSAS CITY'S THIRTIETH ANNUAL ECONOMIC SYMPOSIUM, JACKSON HOLE, WYOMING, AUGUST 25, 2006

Ben S. Bernanke

GLOBAL ECONOMIC INTEGRATION: WHAT'S NEW AND WHAT'S NOT?

When geographers study the earth and its features, distance is one of the basic measures they use to describe the patterns they observe. Distance is an elastic concept, however. The physical distance along a great circle from Wausau, Wisconsin to Wuhan, China is fixed at 7,020 miles. But to an economist, the distance from Wausau to Wuhan can also be expressed in other metrics, such as the cost of shipping goods between the two cities, the time it takes for a message to travel those 7,020 miles, and the cost of sending and receiving the message. Economically relevant distances between Wausau and Wuhan may also depend on what trade economists refer to as the "width of the border," which reflects the extra costs of economic exchange imposed by factors such as tariff and nontariff barriers, as well as costs arising from differences in language, culture, legal traditions, and political systems.

One of the defining characteristics of the world in which we now live is that, by most economically relevant measures, distances are shrinking rapidly.

The shrinking globe has been a major source of the powerful wave of worldwide economic integration and increased economic interdependence that we are currently experiencing. The causes and implications of declining economic distances and increased economic integration are, of course, the subject of this conference.

The pace of global economic change in recent decades has been breathtaking indeed, and the full implications of these developments for all aspects of our lives will not be known for many years. History may provide some guidance, however. The process of global economic integration has been going on for thousands of years, and the sources and consequences of this integration have often borne at least a qualitative resemblance to those associated with the current episode. In my remarks today I will briefly review some past episodes of global economic integration, identify some common themes, and then put forward some ways in which I see the current episode as similar to and different from the past. In doing so, I hope to provide some background and context for the important discussions that we will be having over the next few days.

A Short History of Global Economic Integration

As I just noted, the economic integration of widely separated regions is hardly a new phenomenon. Two thousand years ago, the Romans unified their far-flung empire through an extensive transportation network and a common language, legal system, and currency. One historian recently observed that "a citizen of the empire traveling from Britain to the Euphrates in the mid-second century CE would have found in virtually every town along the journey foods, goods, landscapes, buildings, institutions, laws, entertainment, and sacred elements not dissimilar to those in his own community." (Hitchner, 2003, p. 398). This unification promoted trade and economic development.

A millennium and a half later, at the end of the fifteenth century, the voyages of Columbus, Vasco da Gama, and other explorers initiated a period of trade over even vaster distances. These voyages of discovery were made possible by advances in European ship technology and navigation, including improvements in the compass, in the rudder, and in sail design. The sea lanes opened by these voyages facilitated a thriving intercontinental trade--although the high costs of and the risks associated with long voyages tended to limit trade to a relatively small set of commodities of high value relative to their weight and bulk, such as sugar, tobacco, spices, tea, silk, and precious metals.

Much of this trade ultimately came under the control of the trading companies created by the English and the Dutch. These state-sanctioned monopolies enjoyed--and aggressively protected--high markups and profits. Influenced by the prevailing mercantilist view of trade as a zero-sum game, European nation-states competed to dominate lucrative markets, a competition that sometimes spilled over into military conflict.

The expansion of international trade in the sixteenth century faced some domestic opposition. For example, in an interesting combination of mercantilist thought and social commentary, the reformer Martin Luther wrote in 1524:

"But foreign trade, which brings from Calcutta and India and such places wares like costly silks, articles of gold, and spices--which minister only to ostentation but serve no useful purpose, and which drain away the money of the land and people--would not be permitted if we had proper government and princes... God has cast us Germans off to such an extent that we have to fling our gold and silver into foreign lands and make the whole world rich, while we ourselves remain beggars." (James, 2001, p. 8)

Global economic integration took another major leap forward during the period between the end of the Napoleonic Wars in 1815 and the beginning of World War I. International trade again expanded significantly as did cross-border flows of financial capital and labor. Once again, new technologies played an important role in facilitating integration: Transport costs plunged as steam power replaced the sail and railroads replaced the wagon or the barge, and an ambitious public works project, the opening of the Suez Canal, significantly reduced travel times between Europe and Asia. Communication costs likewise fell as the telegraph came into common use. One observer in the late 1860s described the just completed trans-Atlantic telegraph cable as having "annihilated both space and time in the transmission of intelligence" (Standage, 1998, p. 90). Trade expanded the variety of available goods, both in Europe and elsewhere, and as the trade monopolies of earlier times were replaced by intense competition, prices converged globally for a wide range of commodities, including spices, wheat, cotton, pig iron, and jute (Findlay and O'Rourke, 2002).

The structure of trade during the post-Napoleonic period followed a "core-periphery" pattern. Capital-rich Western European countries, particularly Britain, were the center, or core, of the trading system and the international monetary system. Countries in which natural resources and land were relatively abundant formed the periphery. Manufactured goods, financial capital, and labor tended to flow from the core to the periphery, with natural resources and agricultural products flowing from the periphery to the core. The composition of the core and the periphery remained fairly stable, with one important exception being the United States, which, over the course of the nineteenth century, made the transition from the periphery to the core. The share of manufactured goods in U.S. exports rose from less than 30 percent in 1840 to 60 percent in 1913, and the United States became a net exporter of financial capital beginning in the late 1890s.[1]

For the most part, government policies during this era fostered openness to trade, capital mobility, and migration. Britain unilaterally repealed its tariffs on grains (the so-called corn laws) in 1846, and a series of bilateral treaties subsequently dismantled many barriers to trade in Europe. A growing appreciation for the principle of comparative advantage, as forcefully articulated by Adam Smith and David Ricardo, may have made governments more receptive to the view that international trade is not a zero-sum game but can be beneficial to all participants.

That said, domestic opposition to free trade eventually intensified, as cheap grain from the periphery put downward pressure on the incomes of landowners in the core. Beginning in the late 1870s, many European countries raised tariffs, with Britain being a prominent exception. Britain did respond to protectionist pressures by passing legislation that required that goods be stamped with their country of origin. This step provided additional grist for trade protesters, however, as the author of one British anti-free-trade pamphlet in the 1890s lamented that even the pencil he used to write his protest was marked "made in Germany" (James, 2001, p. 15). In the United States, tariffs on manufactures were raised in the 1860s to relatively high levels, where they remained until well into the twentieth century. Despite these increased barriers to the importation of goods, the United States was remarkably open to immigration throughout this period.

Unfortunately, the international economic integration achieved during the nineteenth century was largely unraveled in the twentieth by two world wars and the Great Depression. After World War II, the major powers undertook the difficult tasks of rebuilding both the physical infrastructure and the international trade and monetary systems. The industrial core--now including an emergent Japan as well as the United States and Western Europe--ultimately succeeded in restoring a substantial degree of economic integration, though decades passed before trade as a share of global output reached pre-World War I levels.

One manifestation of this re-integration was the rise of so-called intra-industry trade. Researchers in the late-1960s and the 1970s noted that an increasing share of global trade was taking place between countries with similar resource endowments, trading similar types of goods--mainly manufactured products traded among industrial countries.[2] Unlike international trade in the nineteenth century, these flows could not be readily explained by the perspectives of Ricardo or of the Swedish economists Eli Heckscher and Bertil Ohlin that emphasized national differences in endowments of natural resources or factors of production. In influential work, Paul Krugman and others have since argued that intra-industry trade can be attributed to firms' efforts to exploit economies of scale, coupled with a taste for variety by purchasers.

Postwar economic re-integration was supported by several factors, both technological and political. Technological advances further reduced the costs of transportation and communication, as the air freight fleet was converted from propeller to jet and intermodal shipping techniques (including containerization) became common. Telephone communication expanded, and digital electronic computing came into use. Taken together, these advances allowed an ever-broadening set of products to be traded internationally. In the policy sphere, tariff barriers--which had been dramatically increased during the Great Depression--were lowered, with many of these reductions negotiated within the multilateral framework provided by the General Agreement on Tariffs and Trade. Globalization was, to some extent, also supported by geopolitical considerations, as economic integration among the Western market economies became viewed as part of the strategy for waging the Cold War. However, although trade expanded significantly in the early post-World War II period, many countries--recalling the exchange-rate and financial crises of the 1930s--adopted regulations aimed at limiting the mobility of financial capital across national borders.

Several conclusions emerge from this brief historical review. Perhaps the clearest conclusion is that new technologies that reduce the costs of transportation and communication have been a major factor supporting global economic integration. Of course, technological advance is itself affected by the economic incentives for inventive activity; these incentives increase with the size of the market, creating something of a virtuous circle. For example, in the nineteenth century, the high potential return to improving communications between Europe and the United States prompted intensive work to better understand electricity and to improve telegraph technology--efforts that together helped make the trans-Atlantic cable possible.

A second conclusion from history is that national policy choices may be critical determinants of the extent of international economic integration.

Britain's embrace of free trade and free capital flows helped to catalyze international integration in the nineteenth century. Fifteenth-century China provides an opposing example. In the early decades of that century, the Chinese sailed great fleets to the ports of Asia and East Africa, including ships much larger than those that the Europeans were to use later in the voyages of discovery. These expeditions apparently had only limited economic impact, however. Ultimately, internal political struggles led to a curtailment of further Chinese exploration (Findlay, 1992). Evidently, in this case, different choices by political leaders might have led to very different historical outcomes.

A third observation is that social dislocation, and consequently often social resistance, may result when economies become more open. An important source of dislocation is that--as the principle of comparative advantage suggests--the expansion of trade opportunities tends to change the mix of goods that each country produces and the relative returns to capital and labor. The resulting shifts in the structure of production impose costs on workers and business owners in some industries and thus create a constituency that opposes the process of economic integration. More broadly, increased economic interdependence may also engender opposition by stimulating social or cultural change, or by being perceived as benefiting some groups much more than others.

The Current Episode of Global Economic Integration

How does the current wave of global economic integration compare with previous episodes? In a number of ways, the remarkable economic changes that we observe today are being driven by the same basic forces and are having similar effects as in the past. Perhaps most important, technological advances continue to play an important role in facilitating global integration. For example, dramatic improvements in supply-chain management, made possible by advances in communication and computer technologies, have significantly reduced the costs of coordinating production among globally distributed suppliers.

Another common feature of the contemporary economic landscape and the experience of the past is the continued broadening of the range of products that are viewed as tradable. In part, this broadening simply reflects the wider range of goods available today--high-tech consumer goods, for example--as well as ongoing declines in transportation costs. Particularly striking, however, is the extent to which information and communication technologies now facilitate active international trade in a wide range of services, from call center operations to sophisticated financial, legal, medical, and engineering services.

The critical role of government policy in supporting, or at least permitting, global economic integration, is a third similarity between the past and the present. Progress in trade liberalization has continued in recent decades--though not always at a steady pace, as the recent Doha Round negotiations demonstrate. Moreover, the institutional framework supporting global trade, most importantly the World Trade Organization, has expanded and strengthened over time. Regional frameworks and agreements, such as the North American Free Trade Agreement and the European Union's "single market," have also promoted trade. Government restrictions on international capital flows have generally declined, and the "soft infrastructure" supporting those flows--for example, legal frameworks and accounting rules--have improved, in part through international cooperation.

In yet another parallel with the past, however, social and political opposition to rapid economic integration has also emerged. As in the past, much of this opposition is driven by the distributional impact of changes in the pattern of production, but other concerns have been expressed as well--for example, about the effects of global economic integration on the environment or on the poorest countries.

What, then, is new about the current episode? Each observer will have his or her own perspective, but, to me, four differences between the current wave of global economic integration and past episodes seem most important. First, the scale and pace of the current episode is unprecedented. For example, in recent years, global merchandise exports have been above 20 percent of world gross domestic product, compared with about 8 percent in 1913 and less than 15 percent as recently as 1990; and international financial flows have expanded even more quickly.[3] But these data understate the magnitude of the change that we are now experiencing. The emergence of China, India, and the former communist-bloc countries implies that the greater part of the earth's population is now engaged, at least potentially, in the global economy. There are no historical antecedents for this development. Columbus's voyage to the New World ultimately led to enormous economic change, of course, but the full integration of the New and the Old Worlds took centuries. In contrast, the economic opening of China, which began in earnest less than three decades ago, is proceeding rapidly and, if anything, seems to be accelerating.

Second, the traditional distinction between the core and the periphery is becoming increasingly less relevant, as the mature industrial economies and the emerging-market economies become more integrated and interdependent.

Notably, the nineteenth-century pattern, in which the core exported manufactures to the periphery in exchange for commodities, no longer holds, as an increasing share of world manufacturing capacity is now found in emerging markets. An even more striking aspect of the breakdown of the core-periphery paradigm is the direction of capital flows: In the nineteenth century, the country at the center of the world's economy, Great Britain, ran current account surpluses and exported financial capital to the periphery. Today, the world's largest economy, that of the United States, runs a current-account deficit, financed to a substantial extent by capital exports from emerging-market nations.

Third, production processes are becoming geographically fragmented to an unprecedented degree.[4] Rather than producing goods in a single process in a single location, firms are increasingly breaking the production process into discrete steps and performing each step in whatever location allows them to minimize costs. For example, the U.S. chip producer AMD locates most of its research and development in California; produces in Texas, Germany, and Japan; does final processing and testing in Thailand, Singapore, Malaysia, and China; and then sells to markets around the globe. To be sure, international production chains are not entirely new: In 1911, Henry Ford opened his company's first overseas factory in Manchester, England, to be closer to a growing source of demand. The factory produced bodies for the Model A automobile, but imported the chassis and mechanical parts from the United States for assembly in Manchester. Although examples like this one illustrate the historical continuity of the process of economic integration, today the geographical extension of production processes is far more advanced and pervasive than ever before. As an aside, some interesting economic questions are raised by the fact that in some cases international production chains are managed almost entirely within a single multinational corporation (roughly 40 percent of U.S. merchandise trade is classified as intra-firm) and in others they are built through arm's-length transactions among unrelated firms. But the empirical evidence in both cases suggests that substantial productivity gains can often be achieved through the development of global supply chains.[5]

The final item on my list of what is new about the current episode is that international capital markets have become substantially more mature. Although the net capital flows of a century ago, measured relative to global output, are comparable to those of the present, gross flows today are much larger. Moreover, capital flows now take many more forms than in the past: In the nineteenth century, international portfolio investments were concentrated in the finance of infrastructure projects (such as the American railroads) and in the purchase of government debt. Today, international investors hold an array of debt instruments, equities, and derivatives, including claims on a broad range of sectors. Flows of foreign direct investment are also much larger relative to output than they were fifty or a hundred years ago.[6] As I noted earlier, the increase in capital flows owes much to capital-market liberalization and factors such as the greater standardization of accounting practices as well as to technological advances.

CONCLUSION

By almost any economically relevant metric, distances have shrunk considerably in recent decades. As a consequence, economically speaking, Wausau and Wuhan are today closer and more interdependent than ever before. Economic and technological changes are likely to shrink effective distances still further in coming years, creating the potential for continued improvements in productivity and living standards and for a reduction in global poverty.

Further progress in global economic integration should not be taken for granted, however. Geopolitical concerns, including international tensions and the risks of terrorism, already constrain the pace of worldwide economic integration and may do so even more in the future. And, as in the past, the social and political opposition to openness can be strong. Although this opposition has many sources, I have suggested that much of it arises because changes in the patterns of production are likely to threaten the livelihoods of some workers and the profits of some firms, even when these changes lead to greater productivity and output overall. The natural reaction of those so affected is to resist change, for example, by seeking the passage of protectionist measures. The challenge for policymakers is to ensure that the benefits of global economic integration are sufficiently widely shared--for example, by helping displaced workers get the necessary training to take advantage of new opportunities--that a consensus for welfare-enhancing change can be obtained. Building such a consensus may be far from easy, at both the national and the global levels. However, the effort is well worth making, as the potential benefits of increased global economic integration are large indeed.

REFERENCES

[16] Bloom, Nick, Raffaella Sadun & John Van Reenen. (2006). "*It Ain't What You Do It's the Way That You Do I.T.--Investigating the Productivity Miracle Using the Overseas Activities of U.S. Multinationals*," unpublished paper, Centre for Economic Performance, March.

[17] Bordo, Michael, Barry Eichengreen & Douglas Irwin. (1999). *"Is Globalization Today Really Different than Globalization a Hundred Years Ago?"* NBER Working Paper No. 7195, June.

[18] Corrado, Carol, Paul Lengermann & Larry Slifman. (2005). "*The Contribution of MNCs to U.S. Productivity Growth, 1977-2000*," unpublished paper, Board of Governors of the Federal Reserve System, July.

[19] Criscuolo, Chiara & Ralf Martin. (2005). *"Multinationals and U.S. Productivity Leadership: Evidence from Great Britain* Centre for Economic Performance, Discussion Paper No. 672, January.

[20] Doms, Mark E. & Bradford Jensen, J. (1998). "Comparing Wages, Skills, and Productivity between Domestically and Foreign-Owned Manufacturing Establishments in the United States," in R.E. Baldwin, R.E. Lipsey, and J. David Richardson, eds., *Geography and Ownership as Bases for Economic Accounting*, *NBER Studies in Income and Wealth,* vol. *59*, Chicago, Ill.: University of Chicago Press, 235-58.

[21] Findlay, Ronald. (1992). "The Roots of Divergence: Western Economic History in Comparative Perspective," *AEA Papers and Proceedings*, vol. *82*, 2, May,158-61.

[22] Findlay, Ronald & Kevin O'Rourke. (2002). *"Commodity Market Integration 1500-2000,"* Centre for Economic Policy Research, Discussion Paper No. 3125, January.

[23] Grubel, Herbert & Lloyd, P. J. (1975). *Intra-Industry Trade*, New York, New York: John Wiley & Sons.

[24] Hanson, Gordon, Raymond Mataloni & Matthew Slaughter. (2005). "Vertical Production Networks in Multinational Firms," *Review of Economics and Statistics*, vol. *87*, 4, November.

[25] Historical Statistics of the United States: Earliest Times to Present (Millennial Edition). (2006). New York, New York: Cambridge University Press.

[26] Hitchner, Bruce. (2003). "Roman Empire," in Joel Mokyr ed., *The Oxford Encyclopedia of Economic History*, Oxford, England: Oxford

University Press, vol. *4*, 397-400.
[27] James, Harold. (2001) *The End of Globalization: Lessons from the Great Depression*, Cambridge, Massachusetts: Harvard University Press.
[28] Kurz, Christopher. (2006). *"Outstanding Outsourcers: A Firm- and Plant-Level Analysis of Production Sharing,"* Finance and Economics Discussion Series 2006-04, Federal Reserve Board, March.
[29] Maddison, Angus. (2001). *The World Economy: A Millenial Perspective*, Paris, France: OECD Development Centre.
[30] Standage, Tom. (1998). *The Victorian Internet*, New York, New York: Walker Publishing Company.

End Notes

[1] Data are from *Historical Statistics of the United States* (2006).
[2] See, for example, Grubel and Lloyd (1975).
[3] Maddison (2001) and International Monetary Fund data.
[4] See, for example, Hanson, Mataloni, and Slaughter (2005).
[5] Some of the key empirical papers in this literature are Doms and Jensen (1998); Criscuolo and Martin (2005); Corrado, Lengermann, and Slifman (2005); Bloom, Sadun, and Van Reenen (2006), and Kurz (2006).
[6] See, for example, Bordo, Eichengreen, and Irwin (1999).

In: Bernanke and Greenspan
Editors R. Anderson, et al.
ISBN: 978-1-62100- 912-2

Chapter 7

Reflections on Central Banking: At a Symposium Sponsored by the Federal Reserve Bank of Kansas City, Jackson Hole, Wyoming, August 26, 2005

Alan Greenspan

In the spirit of this conference, I asked myself what developments in the past eighteen years--both in the economy and in the economics profession--were most important in changing the way we at the Federal Reserve have approached and implemented monetary policy.

The Federal Reserve System was created in 1913 to counter the recurrent credit stringencies that had so frequently been experienced in earlier decades. As lender of last resort, we had a mandate that, at least viewed from today's perspective, was limited. We did not engage in Systemwide open market operations until the 1920s. And as recently as the 1950s, the framework within which those open market operations were formulated was still being developed. Credit was eased when the economy weakened and tightened when inflation threatened, but largely in an ad hoc manner. As a consequence, the Federal Reserve was perceived by some as often accentuating, rather than damping, cycles in prices and activity. Importantly, however, the surge in prices that followed the removal of wage and price controls after World War II and again after the Korean War kept monetary policymakers wary of the threat of inflation.

But concern that the monetary restraint of the 1950s had led to unnecessarily high unemployment persuaded the Federal Open Market Committee to adopt a more stimulative policy stance in the mid-1960s. Those actions appear to have been predicated, in part, on an acceptance of the then-prevalent view that a long-term tradeoff existed between inflation and unemployment.[1]

Subsequently, however, the experience of stagflation in the 1970s and intellectual advances in understanding the importance of expectations--which built on the earlier work of Friedman and Phelps--undermined the notion of a long-run tradeoff.[2] Inflation again became widely viewed as being detrimental to financial stability and macroeconomic performance. And as the decade progressed, a keener appreciation for the monetary roots of inflation emerged both in the profession at large and at central banks. Indeed, the insights from the work of Friedman and Schwartz a decade earlier gained greater prominence in the realm of practical policy.[3]

These events, both economic and intellectual, significantly influenced the tool kits employed by macroeconomists inside and outside policymaking institutions. The large-scale macromodels that had been the focus of so much work in the 1960s came under attack on two fronts.

Most prominently, greater recognition of the importance of expectations suggested that those models, which for the most part incorporated autoregressive expectations, were excessively reduced-form and backward-looking in nature and thus insensitive to changes in economic structure and the policy process. In addition, some researchers observed that simple time-series models often produced better forecasts than the large macromodels of that period.[4]

One prescription was to focus on uncovering, at a more fundamental level, the structural parameters of the economy. Needless to say, this task has proven to be a very tall order that has yet to be filled. Partly in response to these difficulties, a substantial body of research focused on improvements in empirical modeling, such as vector autoregressions for forecasting, and in some cases, for policy analysis.

Each one of these approaches has proven useful, and their descendants are currently employed in various forms in central banks throughout the world. But as yet, none of these approaches is capable of addressing the full range of policymakers' needs.

At various points in time, some analysts have held out hope that a single indicator variable--such as commodity prices, the yield curve, nominal income, and of course, the monetary aggregates--could be used to reliably guide the conduct of monetary policy. If it were the case that an indicator variable or a relatively simple equation could extract the essence of key economic relationships from an exceedingly complex and dynamic real world, then broader issues of economic causality could be set aside, and the tools of policy could be directed at fostering a path for this variable consistent with the attainment of the ultimate policy objective.

M1 was the focus of policy for a brief period in the late 1970s and early 1980s. That episode proved key to breaking the inflation spiral that had developed over the 1970s, but policymakers soon came to question the viability over the longer haul of targeting the monetary aggregates. The relationships of the monetary aggregates to income and prices were eroded significantly over the course of the 1980s and into the early 1990s by financial deregulation, innovation, and globalization. For example, the previously stable relationship of M2 to nominal gross domestic product and the opportunity cost of holding M2 deposits underwent a major structural shift in the early 1990s because of the increasing prevalence of competing forms of intermediation and financial instruments.

In the absence of a single variable, or at most a few, that can serve as a reliable guide, policymakers have been forced to fall back on an approach that entails the interpretation of the full range of economic and financial data. Policy is implemented through nominal and, implicitly, real short-term interest rates. However, reflecting the progress in economic understanding, our actions are now better informed about the pitfalls associated with relying on nominal interest rates to set policy and the important role played by inflation expectations in gauging the stance of monetary policy.

Our appreciation of the importance of expectations has also shaped our increasing transparency about policy actions and their rationale. We have moved toward greater transparency at a "measured pace" in part because we were concerned about potential feedback on the policy process and about being misinterpreted--as indeed we were from time to time. I do not intend this brief and necessarily incomplete review of events to illustrate how far we have come or to despair of how far we have to go. Rather, I believe it demonstrates the inevitable and ongoing uncertainty faced by policymakers.

Despite extensive efforts to capture and quantify what we perceive as the key macroeconomic relationships, our knowledge about many critical linkages is far from complete and, in all likelihood, will remain so. Every model, no matter how detailed or how well conceived, designed, and implemented, is a vastly simplified representation of the world, with all of the intricacies we experience on a day-to-day basis.

Formal models are a necessary, but not sufficient, system of analysis. To be sure, models discipline forecasts by requiring, among many restraints, that identities are indeed equal, inventories non-negative, and marginal propensities to consume positive. But we all temper the outputs of our models and test their results against the ongoing evaluations of a whole array of observations that we do not capture in either the data input or the structure of our models. We are particularly sensitive to observations that appear inconsistent with the causal relationships of our formal models. Tentative revisions of that structure are reflected in our add factors.

Given our inevitably incomplete knowledge about key structural aspects of an ever-changing economy and the sometimes asymmetric costs or benefits of particular outcomes, the paradigm on which we have settled has come to involve, at its core, crucial elements of risk management. In this approach, a central bank needs to consider not only the most likely future path for the economy but also the distribution of possible outcomes about that path. The decisionmakers then need to reach a judgment about the probabilities, costs, and benefits of various possible outcomes under alternative choices for policy.

The risk-management approach has gained greater traction as a consequence of the step-up in globalization and the technological changes of the 1990s, which found us adjusting to events without the comfort of relevant history to guide us. Forecasts of change in the global economic structure--for that is what we are now required to construct--can usefully be described only in probabalistic terms. In other words, point forecasts need to be supplemented by a clear understanding of the nature and magnitude of the risks that surround them.

In effect, we strive to construct a spectrum of forecasts from which, at least conceptually, specific policy action is determined through the tradeoffs implied by a loss-function. In the summer of 2003, for example, the Federal Open Market Committee viewed as very small the probability that the then-gradual decline in inflation would accelerate into a more consequential deflation. But because the implications for the economy were so dire should that scenario play out, we chose to counter it with unusually low interest rates.

The product of a low-probability event and a potentially severe outcome was judged a more serious threat to economic performance than the higher inflation that might ensue in the more probable scenario. Moreover, the risk of a sizable jump in inflation seemed limited at the time, largely because increased productivity growth was resulting in only modest advances in unit labor costs and because heightened competition, driven by globalization, was limiting employers' ability to pass through those cost increases into prices.

Given the potentially severe consequences of deflation, the expected benefits of the unusual policy action were judged to outweigh its expected costs.

The structure of our economy will doubtless change in the years ahead. In particular, our analysis of economic developments almost surely will need to deal in greater detail with balance sheet considerations than was the case in the earlier decades of the postwar period. The determination of global economic activity in recent years has been influenced importantly by capital gains on various types of assets, and the liabilities that finance them. Our forecasts and hence policy are becoming increasingly driven by asset price changes.

The steep rise in the ratio of household net worth to disposable income in the mid-1990s, after a half-century of stability, is a case in point. Although the ratio fell with the collapse of equity prices in 2000, it has rebounded noticeably over the past couple of years, reflecting the rise in the prices of equities and houses.

Whether the currently elevated level of the wealth-to-income ratio will be sustained in the longer run remains to be seen. But arguably, the growing stability of the world economy over the past decade may have encouraged investors to accept increasingly lower levels of compensation for risk. They are exhibiting a seeming willingness to project stability and commit over an ever more extended time horizon.

The lowered risk premiums--the apparent consequence of a long period of economic stability--coupled with greater productivity growth have propelled asset prices higher.[5] The rising prices of stocks, bonds and, more recently, of homes, have engendered a large increase in the market value of claims which, when converted to cash, are a source of purchasing power. Financial intermediaries, of course, routinely convert capital gains in stocks, bonds, and homes into cash for businesses and households to facilitate purchase transactions.[6] The conversions have been markedly facilitated by the financial innovation that has greatly reduced the cost of such transactions.

Thus, this vast increase in the market value of asset claims is in part the indirect result of investors accepting lower compensation for risk. Such an increase in market value is too often viewed by market participants as structural and permanent. To some extent, those higher values may be reflecting the increased flexibility and resilience of our economy. But what they perceive as newly abundant liquidity can readily disappear. Any onset of increased investor caution elevates risk premiums and, as a consequence, lowers asset values and promotes the liquidation of the debt that supported higher asset prices. This is the reason that history has not dealt kindly with the aftermath of protracted periods of low risk premiums.

Broad economic forces are continuously at work, shaping the environment in which the Federal Reserve makes monetary policy. In recent years, the U.S. economy has prospered notably from the increase in productivity growth that began in the mid-1990s and the enhanced competition engendered by globalization. Innovation, spurred by competition, has nurtured the continual scrapping of old technologies to make way for the new. Standards of living have risen because depreciation and other cash flows generated by industries employing older, increasingly obsolescent technologies have been reinvested to finance newly produced capital assets that embody cutting-edge technologies.

But there is also no doubt that this transition to the new high-tech economy, of which expanding global trade is a part, is proving difficult for a segment of our workforce that interfaces day by day with our rapidly changing capital stock. This difficulty is most evident in the increased fear of job-skill obsolescence that has induced significant numbers of our population to resist the competitive pressures inherent in globalization from workers in the major newly emerging market economies. It is important that these understandable fears be addressed through education and training and not by restraining the competitive forces that are so essential to overall rising standards of living of the great majority of our population. A fear of the changes necessary for economic progress is all too evident in the current stymieing of international trade negotiations. Fear of change is also reflected in a hesitancy to face up to the difficult choices that will be required to resolve our looming fiscal problems.

The developing protectionism regarding trade and our reluctance to place fiscal policy on a more sustainable path are threatening what may well be our most valued policy asset: the increased flexibility of our economy, which has fostered our extraordinary resilience to shocks. If we can maintain an adequate degree of flexibility, some of America's economic imbalances, most notably the large current account deficit and the housing boom, can be rectified by adjustments in prices, interest rates, and exchange rates rather than through more-wrenching changes in output, incomes, and employment.

The more flexible an economy, the greater its ability to self-correct in response to inevitable, often unanticipated, disturbances. That process of correction limits the size and the consequences of cyclical imbalances. Enhanced flexibility provides the advantage of allowing the economy to adjust automatically, reducing the reliance on the actions of monetary and other policymakers, which have often come too late or been misguided.

In fact, the performance of the U.S. economy in recent years, despite shocks that in the past would have surely produced marked economic contraction, offers the clearest evidence that we have benefited from an enhanced resilience and flexibility.

We weathered a decline on October 19, 1987 of a fifth of the market value of U.S. equities with little evidence of subsequent macroeconomic stress--an episode that provided an early hint that adjustment dynamics might be changing. The credit crunch of the early 1990s and the bursting of the stock market bubble in 2000 were absorbed with the shallowest recessions in the post-World War II period. And the economic fallout from the tragic events of September 11, 2001, was limited by market forces, with severe economic weakness evident for only a few weeks. Most recently, the flexibility of our market-driven economy has allowed us, thus far, to weather reasonably well the steep rise in spot and futures prices for crude oil and natural gas that we have experienced over the past two years.

This morning I have tried to outline my perceptions of the key developments that have influenced the conduct of monetary policy over the past eighteen years. I acknowledge that monetary policy itself has been an important contributor to the decline in inflation and inflation expectations over the past quarter-century. Indeed, the Federal Reserve under Paul Volcker's leadership starting in 1979 did the very heavy lifting against inflation. The major contribution of the Federal Reserve to fashioning the events of the past decade or so, I believe, was to recognize that the U.S. and global economies were evolving in profound ways and to calibrate inflation-containing policies to gain most effectively from those changes.

For reasons that may not be too obscure, I will pay close attention to, and hope to learn from, the deliberations of the next couple of days. I have been asked to make a few closing remarks tomorrow about some of the unresolved challenges facing policymakers in the years ahead and about my experiences living inside the Federal Reserve for nearly two decades, after so many years of observing our institution from afar.

End Notes

[1] See Romer, Christina D. and David H. Romer, *"The Evolution of Economic Understanding and Postwar Stabilization Policy,"* NBER Working Paper No. 9274 (October 2002), p. 39. *Return to text*

Nearer term, the housing boom will inevitably simmer down. As part of that process, house turnover will decline from currently historic levels, while home price increases will slow and prices could even decrease. As a consequence, home equity extraction will ease and with it some of the strength in personal consumption expenditures. The estimates of how much differ widely.

The surprisingly high correlation between increases in home equity extraction and the current account deficit suggests that an end to the housing boom could induce a significant rise in the personal saving rate, a decline in imports, and a corresponding improvement in the current account deficit. Whether those adjustments are wrenching will depend, as I suggested yesterday, on the degree of economic flexibility that we and our trading partners maintain, and I hope enhance, in the years ahead.

On monetary policy, I envision a continuous refinement of our risk-management paradigm. I presume maximum sustainable economic growth will continue to be our goal, with price stability pursued as a necessary condition to promote that goal. To date, we have chosen not to formulate explicit inflation targets, in part, out of concern that they could inhibit the effective pursuit of our goal.

I remain unpersuaded that explicit numerical inflation targets are a key characteristic that distinguishes behavior among the world's central banks. Despite the various public characterizations of the form of monetary policy regime, the Federal Reserve and most other central banks generally pursue price stability and, consistent with that goal, ease when economic conditions soften and tighten when they firm. That said, I am certain this will remain a topic of lively discussion here and at other monetary forums in years to come. Participants on all sides of that debate will be well served by keeping open minds and remaining attentive to the evidence as events unfold and practices evolve.

Debates on the relative merits of asset price targeting also will continue and possibly intensify in the years ahead. The configuration of asset prices is already an integral part of our evaluation of the large array of forces that influence financial stability and economic growth. But given our current state of knowledge, I find it difficult to envision central banks successfully targeting asset prices any time soon. However, I certainly do not rule out that future work could improve our understanding of asset price behavior, and with it, the conduct of monetary policy.

I will miss debates on such topics with members of the Federal Open Market Committee and with the staffs of the Board and the banks. The Federal

Reserve is a remarkable institution. Aside from its technical expertise in supervision and regulation and in overseeing an increasingly complex payments system, it combines for monetary policy an academic sophistication and a market-sensitive understanding that is brought to bear in formulating the tie between instruments and the goals of monetary policy.

Surely difficult challenges lie ahead for the Fed, some undoubtedly of our own making, and others that will be thrust on us by market or other forces. Having been exposed to the inner workings of this extraordinary institution for nearly two decades, I have little doubt that my successors, and theirs, will continue to sustain the leadership of the American financial system in an ever-widening global economy.

In: Bernanke and Greenspan
Editors R. Anderson, et al.
ISBN: 978-1-62100- 912-2

Chapter 9

At a Symposium Sponsored by the Federal Reserve Bank of Kansas City, Jackson Hole, Wyoming, August 27, 2004

Alan Greenspan

Opening Remarks

I am pleased to be here this morning to discuss the economic implications of population aging and to provide a general overview of some of the issues that will be covered in much greater detail over the next two days.

The so-called elderly dependency ratio--the ratio of older adults to younger adults--has been rising in the industrialized world for at least 150 years. The pace of increase slowed greatly with the birth of the baby-boom generation after World War II. But elderly dependency will almost certainly rise more rapidly as that generation reaches retirement age.

The changes projected for the United States are not as dramatic as those projected for other areas--particularly Europe and Japan--but they nonetheless present substantial challenges. The growth rate of the working-age population in the United States is anticipated to slow from about 1 percent per year today to about 1/4 percent per year by 2035. At the same time, the percentage of the population that is over 65 is poised to rise markedly--from about 12 percent today to perhaps 20 percent by 2035.

These anticipated changes in the age structure of the population and workforces of developed countries are largely a consequence of the decline in fertility that occurred after the birth of the baby-boom generation. The fertility rate in the United States, after peaking in 1957 at about 3-1/2 births over a woman's lifetime, fell to less than 2 by the early 1970s and then rose to about 2.1 by 1990.[1] Since then, the fertility rate has remained close to 2.1, the so-called replacement rate--that is, the level of the fertility rate required to hold the population constant in the absence of immigration or changes in longevity.

Fertility rates in Europe, on the whole, and in Japan have fallen far short of the replacement rate. The decrease in the number of children per family since the end of the baby boom, coupled with increases in life expectancy, has inevitably led to a projected increase in the ratio of elderly to working-age population throughout the developed world.

The populations in most developing countries likewise are expected to have a rising median age but to remain significantly younger and doubtless will grow faster than the populations of the developed countries over the foreseeable future. Eventually, declines in fertility rates and increases in longevity may lead to similar issues with aging populations in what is currently the developing world but likely only well after the demographic transition in the United States and other developed nations.

The aging of the population in the United States will significantly affect our fiscal situation. Most observers expect Social Security, under existing law, to be in chronic deficit over the long haul; however, the program is largely defined benefit, and so the scale of the necessary adjustments is limited. The shortfalls in the Medicare program, however, will almost surely be much larger and much more difficult to eliminate. Medicare faces financial pressure not only from the changing composition of the population but also from continually increased per recipient demand for medical services. The combination of rapidly advancing medical technologies and our current system of subsidized third-party payments suggests continued rapid growth in demand, though future Medicare costs are admittedly very difficult to forecast.

Although the sustainability of fiscal initiatives is generally evaluated for convenience in financial terms, sustainability rests, at root, on the level of real resources available to an economy. The resources available to fund the sum of future retirement benefits and the real incomes of the employed will depend, of course, on the growth rate of labor employed plus the growth rate of the productivity of that labor.

The growth rate of the U.S. working-age population is expected to decline substantially over the next two decades and to remain low thereafter. But the fraction of that population that is employed will almost surely be affected by changes in the economic returns to working and, especially for older workers, improvements in health.

Americans are not only living longer but also generally living healthier. Rates of disability for those over 65 years of age have been declining even as the average age of the above-65 population is increasing. This decline in disability rates reflects both improvements in health and changes in technology that accommodate the physical impairments associated with aging. In addition, work is becoming less physically strenuous but more demanding intellectually, continuing a century-long trend toward a more-conceptual and less-physical economic output. For example, in 1900, agricultural and manual laborers composed about three-quarters of the workforce. By 1950, those types of workers accounted for one-half of the workforce, and though still critical to a significant part of our economic value-added, today compose only about one-quarter of our workforce.

To date, however, despite the improving feasibility of work at older ages, Americans have been retiring at younger ages. But rising pressures on retirement incomes and a growing scarcity of experienced labor could eventually reverse that trend.

Of course, immigration, if we choose to expand it, could also lessen the decline of labor force growth in the United States. As the influx of foreign workers that occurred in response to the tight labor markets of the 1990s demonstrated, U.S. immigration does respond to evolving economic conditions. But to fully offset the effects of the decline in fertility, immigration would have to be much larger than almost all current projections assume.

It is thus heightened growth of output per worker that offers the greatest potential for boosting U.S. gross domestic product to a level that would enable future retirees to maintain their expected standard of living without unduly burdening future workers. Productivity gains in the United States have been exceptional in recent years. But, for a country already on the cutting edge of technology to maintain this pace for a protracted period into the future would be without modern precedent. One policy that could enhance the odds of sustaining high levels of productivity growth is to engage in a long overdue upgrading of primary and secondary school education in the United States.

We obviously cannot attribute recent productivity trends to a high level of national saving. Rather, the effectiveness with which we have invested both domestic saving and funds attracted from abroad is the apparent source of our decade-long rise in productivity growth. As I have noted previously, the bipartisan policies of recent decades directed at deregulation and increasing globalization and the innovation that those policies have spurred have markedly improved our ability to channel saving to its most productive uses, and as a byproduct increased the flexibility and the resiliency of the U.S. economy.

It is, of course, difficult to separate rates of return based on the innovations embedded in new equipment from the enhanced returns made available by productive ideas of how to rearrange existing facilities. From an accounting perspective, efficiency gains, broadly defined as multifactor productivity, have accounted for roughly half the growth in labor productivity in recent years. Capital deepening accounts for most of the remainder.

All else being equal, domestic investment would raise future labor productivity and thereby help provide for our aging population. But the incremental benefit of additional investment may itself be affected by aging. With slowed labor force growth, the amount of new equipment that can be used productively could be more limited, and the return to capital investment could decline as a consequence. Yet it is possible that the return to certain types of capital--particularly those embodying new labor-saving technologies--could increase.

Although domestic investment has accounted for only half our recent productivity gains, its contribution has historically been much larger. Should the pace of efficiency gains slow, it would fall to the level of investment to again become the major contributor to productivity gains. Investment, however, cannot occur without saving. But maintaining even a lower rate of capital investment growth will likely require an increased rate of domestic saving because it is difficult to imagine that we can continue indefinitely to borrow saving from abroad at a rate equivalent to 5 percent of U.S. gross domestic product.

A key component of domestic saving in the United States in future decades will be the path of the personal saving rate. That rate will depend on a number of factors, especially the behavior of the members of the baby-boom cohort during their retirement years. Over the post-World War II period, the elderly in the United States, contrary to conventional wisdom, seem to have drawn down their accumulated wealth only modestly. Apparently retirees spend at a lesser rate and save more than is implicit in the notion that savings are built up during the working years to meet retirement needs. Perhaps, people mis-estimate longevity or desire a large cushion of precautionary savings. Moreover, often people bequeath a significant proportion of their savings to their children or others rather than spend it during retirement. If the baby-boom generation continues this pattern, achieving a higher private domestic saving rate is not out of reach. Even so, critical to national saving will be the level of government, specifically federal government, saving.

A doubling of the over-65 population by 2035 will substantially augment unified budget deficits and, accordingly, reduce federal saving unless actions are taken. But *how* these deficit trends are addressed can have profound economic effects. For example, aside from suppressing economic growth and the tax base, financing expected future shortfalls in entitlement trust funds solely through increased payroll taxes would likely exacerbate the problem of reductions in labor supply by diminishing the returns to work. By contrast, policies promoting longer working life could ameliorate some of the potential demographic stresses.

Changes to the age for receiving full retirement benefits or initiatives to slow the growth of Medicare spending could affect retirement decisions, the size of the labor force, and saving behavior. In choosing among the various tax and spending options, policymakers will need to pay careful attention to the likely economic effects.

The relative aging of the population is bound to bring with it many changes to the economy of the United States--some foreseeable, many probably not. Inevitably it will again require making difficult policy choices to balance competing claims. The decade-long acceleration in productivity and economic growth has seemingly muted the necessity of making such choices. But, as I noted earlier, history discourages the notion that the pace of growth will continue to increase. Though the challenges of prospective increasingly stark choices for the United States seem great, the necessary adjustments will likely be smaller than those required in most other developed countries. But how and when we adjust will also matter.

Early initiatives to address the economic effects of baby-boom retirements could smooth the transition to a new balance between workers and retirees. As a nation, we owe it to our retirees to promise only the benefits that can be delivered. If we have promised more than our economy has the ability to deliver to retirees without unduly diminishing real income gains of workers, as I fear we may have, we must recalibrate our public programs so that pending retirees have time to adjust through other channels. If we delay, the adjustments could be abrupt and painful. Because curbing benefits once bestowed has proved so difficult in the past, fiscal policymakers must be especially vigilant to create new benefits only when their sustainability under the most adverse projections is virtually ensured.

Responding to the pending dramatic rise in dependency ratios will be exceptionally challenging for the policymakers in developed countries. While I do not underestimate the difficulties that we face in the United States, I believe that, given the political will, we are better positioned than most others to make the necessary adjustments.

Aside from the comparatively lesser depth of required adjustment, our open labor markets should respond more easily to the changing needs and abilities of our population; our capital markets should allow for the creation and rapid adoption of new labor-saving technologies, and our open society should be receptive to immigrants. These supports should help us adjust to the inexorabilities of an aging population. Nonetheless, tough policy choices lie ahead.

End Notes

[1] The fertility rate used here is the total fertility rate. It is measured as the average number of children who would be born to a woman over her lifetime if she experienced the birth rates by age observed in any given year.

In: Bernanke and Greenspan
Editors R. Anderson, et al.
ISBN: 978-1-62100- 912-2

Chapter 10

AT A SYMPOSIUM SPONSORED BY THE FEDERAL RESERVE BANK OF KANSAS CITY, JACKSON HOLE, WYOMING, AUGUST 29, 2003

Alan Greenspan

MONETARY POLICY UNDER UNCERTAINTY

Uncertainty is not just an important feature of the monetary policy landscape; it is the defining characteristic of that landscape. As a consequence, the conduct of monetary policy in the United States at its core involves crucial elements of risk management, a process that requires an understanding of the many sources of risk and uncertainty that policymakers face and the quantifying of those risks when possible. It also entails devising, in light of those risks, a strategy for policy directed at maximizing the probabilities of achieving over time our goal of price stability and the maximum sustainable economic growth that we associate with it.

Toward that objective, we have drawn on the work of analysts who over the past half century have devoted much effort to improving our understanding of the economy and its monetary transmission mechanism. A critical result has been the identification of a relatively small set of key relationships that, taken together, provide a useful approximation of our economy's dynamics. Such an approximation underlies the statistical models that we at the Federal Reserve employ to assess the likely influence of our policy decisions.

Despite the extensive efforts to capture and quantify these key macroeconomic relationships, our knowledge about many of the important linkages is far from complete and in all likelihood will always remain so. Every model, no matter how detailed or how well designed conceptually and empirically, is a vastly simplified representation of the world that we experience with all its intricacies on a day-to-day basis. Consequently, even with large advances in computational capabilities and greater comprehension of economic linkages, our knowledge base is barely able to keep pace with the ever-increasing complexity of our global economy.

Given this state of flux, it is apparent that a prominent shortcoming of our structural models is that, for ease in parameter estimation, not only are economic responses presumed fixed through time, but they are generally assumed to be linear. An assumption of linearity may be adequate for estimating *average* relationships, but few expect that an economy will respond linearly to every aberration. Although some nonlinearities are accounted for in our modeling exercises, we cannot be certain that our simulations provide reasonable approximations of the economy's behavior in times of large idiosyncratic shocks.

Recent history has also reinforced the perception that the relationships underlying the economy's structure change over time in ways that are difficult to anticipate. This has been most apparent in the changing role of our standard measure of the money stock. Because an interest rate, by definition, is the exchange rate for money against non-monies, money obviously is central to monetary policy. However, in the past two decades, what constitutes money has been obscured by the introduction of technologies that have facilitated the proliferation of financial products and have altered the empirical relationship between economic activity and what we define as money, and in doing so has inhibited the keying of monetary policy to the control of the measured money stock.[1]

Another example of ongoing structural change relates to innovations in mortgage finance. This includes the elimination of Regulation Q, the emergence of variable rate loans, the growth of the mortgage-backed securities market, and improvements in the efficiency of the credit application process. These developments appear to have buffered activity in the housing market to some extent from shifts in monetary policy. But some of the same innovations in housing finance have opened new avenues of policy influence on economic behavior. For example, households have been able with increasing ease to extract equity from their homes, and this doubtless has helped support consumer spending in recent years, complementing the traditional effects of monetary policy.

What then are the implications of this largely irreducible uncertainty for the conduct of monetary policy? A well-known proposition is that, under a very restrictive set of assumptions, uncertainty has no bearing on the actions that policymakers might choose, and so they should proceed as if they know the precise structure of the economy.[2] These assumptions--linearity in the structure of the economy, perfect knowledge of the interest-sensitivity of aggregate spending and other so-called slope parameters, and a very specific attitude of policymakers toward risk--are never met in the real world.

Indeed, given our inevitably incomplete knowledge about key structural aspects of our ever-changing economy and the sometimes asymmetric costs or benefits of particular outcomes, a central bank seeking to maximize its probability of achieving its goals is driven, I believe, to a risk-management approach to policy. By this I mean that policymakers need to consider not only the most likely future path for the economy but also the distribution of possible outcomes about that path. They then need to reach a judgment about the probabilities, costs, and benefits of the various possible outcomes under alternative choices for policy.

A policy action that is calculated to be optimal based on a simulation of one particular model may not, in fact, be optimal once the full extent of uncertainty in the policymaking environment is taken into account. In general, it is entirely possible that different policies will exhibit different degrees of robustness with respect to the true underlying structure of the economy. For example, policy A might be judged as best advancing the policymakers' objectives, conditional on a particular model of the economy, but might also be seen as having relatively severe adverse consequences if the true structure of the economy turns out to be other than the one assumed. On the other hand, policy B might be somewhat less effective in advancing the policy objectives under the assumed baseline model but might be relatively benign in the event that the structure of the economy turns out to differ from the baseline. These considerations have inclined Federal Reserve policymakers toward policies that limit the risk of deflation even though the baseline forecasts from most conventional models would not project such an event.

At times, policy practitioners operating under a risk-management paradigm may be led to undertake actions intended to provide some insurance against the emergence of especially adverse outcomes. For example, following the Russian debt default in the fall of 1998, the Federal Open Market

Committee (FOMC) eased policy despite our perception that the economy was expanding at a satisfactory pace and that, even without a policy initiative, was likely to continue to do so.[3] We eased policy because we were concerned about the low-probability risk that the default might severely disrupt domestic and international financial markets, with outsized adverse feedback to the performance of the U.S. economy.

The product of a low-probability event and a severe outcome, should it occur, was judged a larger threat than the possible adverse consequences of insurance that might prove unnecessary. The cost--or premium--of the financial-contagion insurance was the associated increase in the risk of higher inflation at some future date. This cost was viewed as relatively low at the time, largely because increased competition, driven by globalization, thwarted employers' ability to pass through higher labor costs into prices. Given the Russian default, the benefits of the unusual policy action were deemed to outweigh its costs.

Such a cost-benefit analysis is an ongoing part of monetary policy decisionmaking, and tips more toward monetary ease when the fallout from a contractionary event such as the Russian default seems increasingly likely and its occurrence seems especially costly. Conversely, in 1979, with inflation threatening to get out of control, the cost to the economy of a major withdrawal of liquidity was judged far less than the potential long-term consequences of leaving accelerating prices unaddressed.

In implementing a risk-management approach to policy, we must confront the fact that only a limited number of risks can be quantified with any confidence. And even these risks are generally quantifiable only if we accept the assumption that the future will replicate the past. Other risks are essentially unquantifiable--representing Knightian uncertainty, if you will--because we may not fully appreciate even the full range of possibilities, let alone each possibility's likelihood. As a result, risk management often involves significant judgment on the part of policymakers, as we evaluate the risks of different events and the probability that our actions will alter those risks.

For such judgment, we policymakers, rather than relying solely on the specific linkages expressed in our formal models, have tended to draw from broader, though less mathematically precise, hypotheses of how the world works. For example, inference of how market participants might respond to a monetary policy initiative may need to reference past behavior during a period only roughly comparable to the current situation.

Some critics have argued that such an approach to policy is too undisciplined--judgmental, seemingly discretionary, and difficult to explain.

The Federal Reserve should, some conclude, attempt to be more formal in its operations by tying its actions solely to the prescriptions of a formal policy rule. That any approach along these lines would lead to an improvement in economic performance, however, is highly doubtful. Our problem is not the complexity of our models but the far greater complexity of a world economy whose underlying linkages appear to be in a continual state of flux.

Rules by their nature are simple, and when significant and shifting uncertainties exist in the economic environment, they cannot substitute for risk-management paradigms, which are far better suited to policymaking. Were we to introduce an interest rate rule, how would we judge the meaning of a rule that posits a rate far above or below the current rate? Should policymakers adjust the current rate to that suggested by the rule? Should we conclude that this deviation is normal variance and disregard the signal? Or should we assume that the parameters of the rule are misspecified and adjust them to fit the current rate? Given errors in our underlying data, coupled with normal variance, we might not know the correct course of action for a considerable time. Partly for these reasons, the prescriptions of formal interest rate rules are best viewed only as helpful adjuncts to policy, as indeed many proponents of policy rules have suggested.

In summary then, monetary policy based on risk management appears to be the most useful regime by which to conduct policy. The increasingly intricate economic and financial linkages in our global economy, in my judgment, compel such a conclusion. Over the next couple of days, we will have the opportunity to consider in greater detail some important changes in our economic and financial systems and their implications for the conduct of monetary policy. As always, I look forward to an engaging discussion.

End Notes

[1] Nonetheless, in the tradition of Milton Friedman, it is difficult to disregard the long-run relationship between money and prices. In particular, since 1959 unit money supply, the ratio of M2 to real GDP, has increased at an annual rate of 3.7 percent and GDP prices have risen 3.8 percent per year. (A consistent time-series for M2 is available back to 1959. Among other changes, deposit data at a daily frequency were incorporated in measures of the monetary aggregates as of that date.).

[2] William Brainard, "Uncertainty and the Effectiveness of Monetary Policy," *American Economic Review,* May 1967, pp. 411-25.

[3] See *minutes of the FOMC meeting of September 29, 1998.*

In: Bernanke and Greenspan
Editors R. Anderson, et al.
ISBN: 978-1-62100- 912-2

Chapter 11

ECONOMIC VOLATILITY: AT A SYMPOSIUM SPONSORED BY THE FEDERAL RESERVE BANK OF KANSAS CITY, JACKSON HOLE, WYOMING, AUGUST 30, 2002

Alan Greenspan

Over the past two decades we have witnessed a remarkable turnaround in the U.S. economy. The aftermath of the Vietnam War and a series of oil shocks had left the United States with high inflation, lackluster productivity growth, and a declining competitive position in international markets.

But rather than accept the role of a once-great, but diminishing economic force, for reasons that will doubtless be debated for years to come, we resurrected the dynamism of previous generations of Americans. A wave of innovation across a broad range of technologies, combined with considerable deregulation and a further lowering of barriers to trade, fostered a pronounced expansion of competition and creative destruction.

The result through the 1990s of all this seeming-heightened instability for individual businesses, somewhat surprisingly, was an apparent *reduction* in the volatility of output and in the frequency and amplitude of business cycles for the macroeconomy. While the empirical evidence on the importance of changes in the magnitude of the shocks impacting on our economy remains ambiguous, it does appear that shocks are more readily absorbed than in decades past. The massive drop in equity wealth over the past two years, the sharp decline in capital investment, and the tragic events of September 11 might reasonably have been expected to produce an immediate severe contraction in the U.S. economy. But this did not occur. Economic imbalances in recent years apparently have been addressed more expeditiously and effectively than in the past, aided importantly by the more widespread availability and more intensive use of real-time information.

But faster adjustments imply a greater volatility in expected corporate earnings. Although direct estimates of investors' expectations for earnings are not readily available, indirect evidence does seem to support an increased volatility in those expectations. Securities analysts' expectations for long-term earnings growth, an assumed proxy for investors' expectations, were revised up significantly over the second half of the 1990s and into 2000.[1] Over that same period, risk spreads on corporate bonds rose markedly on net, implying a rising probability of default. Default, of course, is generally associated with negative earnings. Hence, higher average expected earnings growth coupled with a rising probability of default implies a greater variance of earnings expectations, a consequence of a lengthened negative tail. Consistent with a greater variability of earnings expectations, volatility of stock prices has been elevated in recent years.

The increased volatility of stock prices and the associated quickening of the adjustment process would also have been expected to be accompanied by *less* volatility in real economic variables. And that does appear to have been the case. That is, after all, the purpose of a prompter response by businesses: to prevent severe imbalances from developing at their firms, which in the aggregate can turn into deep contractions if unchecked.

As might be expected, accumulating signs of greater economic stability over the decade of the 1990s fostered an increased willingness on the part of business managers and investors to take risks with both positive and negative consequences. Stock prices rose in response to the greater propensity for risk-taking and to improved prospects for earnings growth that reflected emerging evidence of an increased pace of innovation. The associated decline in the cost of equity capital spurred a pronounced rise in capital investment and productivity growth that broadened impressively in the latter years of the 1990s. Stock prices rose further, responding to the growing optimism about greater stability, strengthening investment, and faster productivity growth.

But, as we indicated in congressional testimony in July 1999,[2] "... productivity acceleration does not ensure that equity prices are not overextended. There can be little doubt that if the nation's productivity growth has stepped up, the level of profits and their future potential would be elevated. That prospect has supported higher stock prices. The danger is that in these circumstances, an unwarranted, perhaps euphoric, extension of recent developments can drive equity prices to levels that are unsupportable even if risks in the future become relatively small. Such straying above fundamentals could create problems for our economy when the inevitable adjustment occurs."

Looking back on those years, it is evident that increased productivity growth imparted significant upward momentum to expectations of earnings growth and, accordingly, to price-earnings ratios. Between 1995 and 2000, the price-earnings ratio of the S&P 500 rose from 15 to nearly 30. However, to attribute that increase entirely to revised earnings expectations would require an upward revision to the growth of real earnings of 2 full percentage points in perpetuity.[3]

Because the real riskless rate of return apparently did not change much during that five-year period, anything short of such an extraordinary permanent increase in the growth of structural productivity, and thus earnings,[4] implies a significant fall in real equity premiums in those years.

If all of the drop in equity premiums had resulted from a permanent reduction in cyclical volatility, stock prices arguably could have stabilized at their levels in the summer of 2000. That clearly did not happen, indicating that stock prices, in fact, had risen to levels in excess of any economically supportable base. Toward the end of that year, expectations for long-term earnings growth began to turn down. At about the same time, equity premiums apparently began to rise.

The consequent reversal in stock prices that has occurred over the past couple of years has been particularly pronounced in the high-tech sectors of the economy. The investment boom in the late 1990s, initially spurred by significant advances in information technology, ultimately produced an overhang of installed capacity. Even though demand for a number of high-tech products was doubling or tripling annually, in many cases new supply was coming on even faster. Overall, capacity in high-tech manufacturing industries rose more than 40 percent in 2000, well in excess of its rapid rate of increase over the previous two years. In light of the burgeoning supply, the pace of increased demand for the newer technologies, though rapid, fell short of that needed to sustain the elevated real rate of return for the whole of the high-tech capital stock. Returns on the securities of high-tech firms ultimately collapsed, as did capital investment. Similar, though less severe, adjustments were occurring in many industries across our economy.

Some decline in equity premiums in the latter part of the 1990s almost surely would have been anticipated as the continuing absence of any business correction reinforced notions of increased secular stability. In such an environment, the relatively mild recession that we experienced in 2001 might still have been expected to leave equity premiums below their long-term averages. That apparently has not been the case, as the tendency toward lower equity premiums created by a more stable economy may have been offset to some extent recently by concerns about the quality of corporate governance.

The struggle to understand developments in the economy and financial markets since the mid-1990s has been particularly challenging for monetary policymakers. We were confronted with forces that none of us had personally experienced. Aside from the then recent experience of Japan, only history books and musty archives gave us clues to the appropriate stance for policy. We at the Federal Reserve considered a number of issues related to asset bubbles--that is, surges in prices of assets to unsustainable levels. As events evolved, we recognized that, despite our suspicions, it was very difficult to definitively identify a bubble until after the fact--that is, when its bursting confirmed its existence. Moreover, it was far from obvious that bubbles, even if identified early, could be preempted short of the central bank inducing a substantial contraction in economic activity--the very outcome we would be seeking to avoid.

Prolonged periods of expansion promote a greater *rational* willingness to take risks, a pattern very difficult to avert by a modest tightening of monetary policy. In fact, our experience over the past fifteen years suggests that monetary tightening that deflates stock prices without depressing economic activity has often been associated with subsequent *increases* in the level of stock prices.

For example, stock prices rose following the completion of the more than 300-basis-point rise in the federal funds rate in the twelve months ending in February 1989. And during the year beginning in February 1994, the Federal Reserve raised the federal funds target 300 basis points. Stock prices initially flattened, but as soon as that round of tightening was completed, they resumed their marked upward advance. From mid-1999 through May 2000, the federal funds rate was raised 150 basis points. However, equity price increases were largely undeterred during that period despite what now, in retrospect, was the exhausted tail of a bull market.[5]

Such data suggest that nothing short of a sharp increase in short-term rates that engenders a significant economic retrenchment is sufficient to check a nascent bubble. The notion that a well-timed incremental tightening could have been calibrated to prevent the late 1990s bubble is almost surely an illusion.

Instead, we noted in the previously cited mid-1999 congressional testimony the need to focus on policies "to mitigate the fallout when it occurs and, hopefully, ease the transition to the next expansion."

It seems reasonable to generalize from our recent experience that no low-risk, low-cost, incremental monetary tightening exists that can reliably deflate a bubble. But is there some policy that can at least limit the size of a bubble and, hence, its destructive fallout? From the evidence to date, the answer appears to be no.[6] But we do need to know more about the behavior of equity premiums and bubbles and their impact on economic activity.[7]

The equity premium, computed as the total expected return on common stocks less that on riskless debt, prices the risk taken by investors in purchasing equities rather than risk-free debt. It is a measure largely of the risk aversion of investors, not that of corporate managers. An increased appetite for risk by investors, for example, is manifested by a shift in their willingness to hold equity in place of psychologically less-stressful, but lower-yielding, debt. In this case, the cost of equity confronting corporate managers falls relative to the cost of debt. With greater access to lower-cost equity, managers are able to finance a higher proportion of riskier real assets with a lessened call on cash flow and fear of default.

Thus, it is generally the changing risk preferences of investors, not of corporate managers, that govern the mix of risk investment in an economy. Managers presumably employ market prices of debt and equity coupled with the calculated rate of return on particular real investment projects to determine the level of corporate investment. To be sure, managers' personal sense of risk aversion can sometimes influence the capital investment process, but it is probably a secondary effect relative to the vagaries of investor psychology.

Bubbles thus appear to primarily reflect exuberance on the part of investors in pricing financial assets. If managers and investors perceived the same degree of risk, and both correctly judged a *sustainable* rise in profits stemming from new technology, for example, none of a rise in stock prices would reflect a bubble. Bubbles appear to emerge when investors either overestimate the sustainable rise in profits or unrealistically lower the rate of discount they apply to expected profits and dividends. The distinction cannot readily be ascertained from market prices. But the equity premium less the expected growth of dividends, and presumed earnings, can be estimated as the dividend yield less the real long-term interest rate on U.S. Treasuries.[8]

If equity premiums were redefined to include both the unrealistic part of profit projections and the unsustainably low segment of discount factors, and if we had associated measures of these concepts, we could employ this measure to infer emerging bubbles. That is, if we could substitute realistic projections of earnings and dividend growth, perhaps based on structural productivity growth and the behavior of the payout ratio, the residual equity premium might afford some evidence of a developing bubble. Of course, if the central bank had access to this information, so would private agents, rendering the development of bubbles highly unlikely.

Bubbles are often precipitated by perceptions of real improvements in the productivity and underlying profitability of the corporate economy. But as history attests, investors then too often exaggerate the extent of the improvement in economic fundamentals. Human psychology being what it is, bubbles tend to feed on themselves, and booms in their later stages are often supported by implausible projections of potential demand. Stock prices and equity premiums are then driven to unsustainable levels.

Certainly, a bubble cannot persist indefinitely. Eventually, unrealistic expectations of future earnings will be proven wrong. As this happens, asset prices will gravitate back to levels that are in line with a sustainable path for earnings. The continual pressing of reality on perception inevitably disciplines the views of both investors and managers.

As I noted earlier, the key policy question is: If low-cost, incremental policy tightening appears incapable of deflating bubbles, do other options exist that can at least effectively limit the size of bubbles without doing substantial damage in the process? To date, we have not been able to identify such policies, though perhaps we or others may do so in the future. It is by no means evident to us that we currently have--or will be able to find--a measure of equity premiums or related indicators that convincingly presage an emerging bubble. Short of such a measure, I find it difficult to conceive of an adequate degree of central bank certainty to justify the scale of preemptive tightening that would likely be necessary to neutralize a bubble.

As we delve deeper into the questions raised by the developments of recent years, the interplay between structural productivity growth and equity premiums, so evident during the past business cycle, is bound to play a prominent role. We need particularly to determine whether the periodic emergence of market bubbles, which have occurred so often in the past, is inevitable going forward. As financial wealth becomes an ever-more-important determinant of activity, we need also to understand far better how changing equity premiums affect and reflect real and financial investment decisions. If the equity premium has so demonstrable an influence on our economies as it appears to have, the value of further investigation of this topic is evident.

In conclusion, the endeavors of policymakers to stabilize our economies require a functioning model of the way our economies work. Increasingly, it appears that this model needs to embody movements in equity premiums and the development of bubbles if it is to explain history.

Any useful model needs to credibly simulate counterfactual alternatives. We must remember that structural models that do a poor job of explaining history presumably also will provide an incomplete basis for policymaking. Often the internal structure of such models has been employed to evaluate the effect of various stabilization policies. But the results from models whose internal structure cannot successfully replicate key features of cyclical behavior must be interpreted carefully. The recent importance of movements in equity premiums and asset bubbles suggests the need to better understand and integrate these concepts into the models used for policy analysis.

I anticipate productive discussion of these and other issues related to stabilization policy over the next couple of days.

End Notes

[1] These are earnings-weighted projections for S&P 500 corporations as reported by securities analysts to I/B/E/S, a financial research firm. The roughly twenty-year history of this series confirms a pronounced upward bias in these long-term projections of analysts of approximately 4 to 5 percentage points in annual expected growth. There is little evidence, however, one way or the other, of bias to *changes* in the rate of growth.

[2] Committee on Banking and Financial Services, U.S. House of Representatives, July 22, 1999.

[3] For continuous discounting over an infinite horizon, $k\ (E/P) = r + b - g$, where k equals the current, and assumed future, dividend payout ratio, E current earnings, P the current stock price, r the riskless interest rate, b the equity premium, and g the growth rate of earnings. The relationship holds for both real and nominal variables. If k is assumed to be 0.6, the average over the second half of the 1990s (taking account of payouts made through share repurchases), a rise in the P/E of the S&P 500 from 15 to 30, with r and b unchanged in real terms, implies an increase in g of 0.02 in real terms.

[4] If earnings are a constant share of output in the long run, then real long-term earnings growth is the product of productivity growth and growth in labor force hours. In this exercise, the growth rate of hours, driven by demographics, is assumed not to change; hence, the growth rates of earnings and productivity are the same.

[5] Stock prices peaked in March 2000, but the market basically moved sideways until September of that year.

[6] Some have asserted that the Federal Reserve can deflate a stock-price bubble--rather painlessly--by boosting margin requirements. The evidence suggests otherwise. First, the amount of margin debt is small, having never amounted to more than about 1-3/4 percent of the market value of equity; moreover, even this figure overstates the amount of margin debt used to

purchase stock, as such debt also finances short-sales of equity and transactions in non-equity securities. Second, investors need not rely on margin debt to take a leveraged position in equities. They can borrow from other sources to buy stock. Or, they can purchase options, which will affect stock prices given the linkages across markets. Thus, not surprisingly, the preponderance of research suggests that changes in margins are not an effective tool for reducing stock market volatility. It is possible that margin requirements inhibit very small investors whose access to other forms of credit is limited. If so, the only effect of raised margin requirements is to price out the very small investor without addressing the broader issue of stock price bubbles. If a change in margin requirements were taken by investors as a signal that the central bank would soon tighten monetary policy enough to burst a bubble, then there might be the appearance of a causal effect. But it is the prospect of monetary policy action, not the margin increase, that should be viewed as the trigger. In a similar manner, history tells us that "jawboning" asset markets will be ineffective unless backed by action.

[7] The sharp stock market contraction on October 19, 1987 of more than one-fifth requires especial further study. Equity prices rose sharply during the spring and summer, again despite the rise in short-term rates through late summer of that year. The price collapse clearly had some of the characteristics of prolonged and far larger bubbles, but stock prices quickly stabilized without significant effect on economic activity. And, in line with later episodes, the failure of the collapse to have an economic impact seems to have contributed to subsequent higher stock prices.

[8] From footnote 3, $k\ (E/P) = D/P = r + b - g$, where D is current dividends. Hence, $D/P - r = b - g$

INDEX

A

B

C

D

E

F

G

H

I